BE SELFISH

Tools & Techniques to Unleash the Enlightened Warrior in YOU

SARAVANAN IPS

ISBN
Paperback 979-8-89363-269-9
Hardcase 979-8-89363-270-5

CONTENTS

PREFACE

*'Self-victimisation precedes self-awareness.
Self-awareness precedes self-reflection.
Self-reflection precedes self-actualisation.'*

In the complex landscape of modern life, everyone is being victimised either directly or indirectly, either ignorantly or voluntarily, and either knowingly or unknowingly in different ways. Society utilises diverse legal, political, economic, educational, and social systems to maintain order and fairness and provide individual welfare. Yet, flaws and biases in these systems can result in victimisation, subjecting individuals to disadvantages or harm stemming from systemic, historical, or societal issues. Changing such systems can prove challenging, but we can change ourselves to ensure that, rather than remaining victims, we achieve our full potential as individuals. The journey from self-victimisation to self-actualisation is a profound transformation that begins with self-awareness. A lack of self-awareness and self-care can indirectly contribute to victimisation. Poor nutrition and insufficient physical activity can negatively impact physical and mental health, making individuals more susceptible to fatigue, low self-esteem, and impaired judgment. Individuals with low emotional awareness may struggle to detect subtle cues that someone or something is manipulative, abusive, or exploitative, making them more likely to fall prey to harmful individuals or environments. Overcoming these obstacles is possible through personal effort and the prioritisation of physical and mental health, allowing us to break free from a mindset of susceptibility and embrace personal empowerment. While it may be easy to point fingers at various aspects of society, the real solution lies in each individual. The journey towards a better world starts with each one of us. Everyone's individual efforts can pave the way for a brighter and more compassionate future.

At the age of 30, a visionary soul took a solemn oath to change the world, driven by boundless passion and noble aspirations. However, as he journeyed through life, he encountered the harsh realities of the world's complexities, and his attempts to bring about significant global change seemed to slip through his grasp.

Undeterred, he pressed on and, at 50, redirected his focus towards his own country, hoping a more localised approach would yield success. Nevertheless, he faced formidable barriers, for the country was a mosaic of diverse races, religions, languages, and cultures, each contributing to its rich tapestry of identity.

Approaching 70, with wisdom born from a lifetime of experiences, he realised that societal transformation must begin at a smaller, more intimate level. He resolved to change his own society, starting with those closest to him and expanding outwards to his immediate community.

Yet, even in his sincerest efforts, the path to change remained arduous. And as he lay on his deathbed, he reflected on his life's journey. In a moment of profound clarity, he understood that the key to bringing about true change was to first improve himself.

Regrettably, he realised that if he had focused on self-improvement from the outset, his positive transformation could have influenced and inspired others more profoundly, rippling through the world in ways he could have never imagined.

With this new found understanding, the visionary soul breathed his last, leaving behind a legacy of growth, introspection, and the profound insight that lasting change begins within oneself.

The above story serves as a poignant reminder that, to change the world, one must first embark on the journey of personal transformation. To effect positive change in the world, one must embrace self-love and prioritise well-being. When we nurture a profound love for ourselves, the path towards making better choices becomes clearer to us.

The Power of Rejuvenation

Undoubtedly, one of the most extraordinary gifts bestowed upon mankind is the innate capacity of the human body for rejuvenation. This phenomenon entails a meticulous and multifaceted process of self-renewal, ensuring our well-being at various levels. At its core, cellular regeneration tirelessly replaces old or damaged cells, thereby preserving the integrity of our tissues and organs.

The human body is an intricate marvel, filled with astonishing capabilities and complexities. Scientific discoveries have revealed that the brain can generate new neurons throughout life in a process called neurogenesis, crucial for learning, memory, and overall brain health. Equally remarkable is the symbiotic relationship between the gut microbiome and cognitive function, emphasising the profound impact of our intestinal microorganisms on digestion, immunity, and well-being. Orchestrating these functions is the body's internal timekeeper, the circadian rhythm, influenced by environmental cues. Interconnectedness takes centre stage as scientists unveil links between gut and brain, liver and eyes, kidneys and ears, lungs and nose, heart and tongue, showcasing the intricate web woven within our biological systems. Beyond these connections, the body's sheer scale is awe-inspiring; it houses trillions of cells and a 60, 000-mile network of blood vessels. From the self-renewal of the skin every 27 days to the stomach's ability to dissolve indigestible items, each fact about how the human body functions contributes to a portrait of an organism capable of adaptation, regeneration, and endurance, constantly evolving through time. The human body is a masterpiece of biological engineering.

Personal transformation is achievable at any life stage when we address fundamental aspects of self-care, particularly nutrition, hydration, air quality, sleep, and mindset. These elements are essential for physical and mental well-being, and making positive changes in these areas can lead to significant personal growth and transformation. These changes can enhance the vitality of every cell in our body, leading to holistic well-being.

Be Holistically Selfish

The idea of being holistically selfish suggests that, by prioritising our own well-being and personal growth, we can become healthier and more balanced individuals. This attitude doesn't mean neglecting others; instead, it emphasises self-care as a foundation for being more effective and beneficial to others, recognising the symbiotic relationship between the two. When you're emotionally, mentally, and physically healthy, when you feel secure and fulfilled, you are more likely to extend compassion, understanding, and support to others, connect with their experiences, and contribute to the building of a harmonious and interconnected community.

Rule Yourself

Under the rule of law, every person and institution, including the government, is subject to established legal principles. Under self-rule, one's conscience assumes the role of the law. Individuals must adhere to their internal moral compass and principles, guiding their actions and decisions. This intrinsic sense of accountability mirrors the broader societal structure, in which adherence to personal values contributes to a collectively just and orderly community, much like the rule of law governs a nation.

Solving our problems is within our control. Meaningful change won't happen unless we take proactive steps to initiate it. The challenges in our lives often stem from our own negative mental programming. To alleviate difficulties, it's essential to eliminate destructive thought patterns that cause suffering and replace them with positive programming that fosters optimistic thinking. This mental reprogramming empowers us to navigate challenges with a more constructive mindset.

For instance, stress and anxiety often result from dwelling on the past or worrying about the future, which is why it's crucial to prioritise living in the present. However, this doesn't mean that we should neglect the valuable lessons we can learn from the past and the necessary planning for the future. The key is to learn from the past but not dwell on it, to live in the present but plan for the future. This balance allows us to use the past as a guide, fully enjoy the present, and prepare for what lies ahead without excessive stress or anxiety.

External influences may attempt to belittle and hurt you, but it's crucial to avoid self-belittlement at all costs. Let your self-compassion and self-esteem stand as protective shields against internal negativity. Self-compassion and self-esteem play a vital role, offering a kinder and more forgiving outlook on one's own mistakes and limitations. In a world full of distractions, dedicating two focused hours daily to productive work with self-control and discipline can lead to significant success. It's about channelling your energy into a targeted and mindful effort.

Early recognition and understanding of one's inner self, coupled with the ability to navigate emotions effectively, significantly enhance the chances of achieving goals and overcoming life's challenges at the earliest.

Elevating Self-awareness and Emotional Awareness

This is a progressive journey in which every action counts. Initially, sidestepping procrastination is pivotal. Advancing, one should review one's daily performance and plan ahead. Moving to the next stage, crafting a to-do list becomes essential. A to-do list should be manageable and the items on it should be listed in order of priority. Employing the time-blocking technique and conducting regular self-reviews constitute the pinnacle of heightened awareness.

Similarly, the journey towards elevated awareness begins with the initial step of rising early in the morning. Progressing to the next stage involves engaging in purposeful physical activity and selecting suitable exercises. Finally, the pinnacle is reached by embracing a nutritious breakfast, completing the sequence of mindful morning routines.

In the realm of thought progression, the journey unfolds by initially observing thoughts. Advancing, one must identify triggers, recognise thinking errors, biases, and impurities in our mindset. Ultimately, the zenith is attained through the cultivation of a growth mindset, completing the transition from destructive to constructive thoughts.

Developing heightened awareness involves progressing through various levels of conscious choices. For instance, initially, one should recognise the adverse effects of unhealthy drinks. Moving to the next level, choosing healthier options becomes crucial. At an advanced stage, the focus shifts to nuanced choices, such as opting for mildly sweet coconut water, as it comes packed with mineral content. The pinnacle lies in savouring each sip of such healthy drinks consciously, embodying a state of heightened awareness and present-moment enjoyment.

The progression towards heightened self-realisation unfolds through distinct phases. Initially, in the Ignorance phase, one may grapple with self-victimisation and self-imposed limitations. Transitioning into the Awareness phase marks a pivotal shift that involves embracing self-awareness, self-introspection, and self-reflection. The focus broadens in the Advancing phase, encompassing self-motivation, self-discipline, self-compassion, self-responsibility, self-care, self-esteem, and self-hygiene. The journey intensifies in the Acceleration phase, where self-mastery, self-management, self-sufficiency, and self-assertiveness take centre-stage. Finally, reaching the Peak Performance phase signifies the culmination of self-actualisation and self-realisation, embodying the zenith of heightened self-awareness.

Self-Questioning

Self-questioning encourages individuals to assess their actions and decisions, driving self-awareness and personal growth rather than self-affirmation. Self-questioning is a powerful tool for self-actualisation. It can help us understand ourselves better, make better decisions, and achieve our peak performance. By asking ourselves questions, we can become more aware of our health, thoughts, feelings, strengths, and limitations. This can help us make better decisions and take actions that are aligned with our values and goals. Self-questioning can help us challenge our assumptions and biases and consider different perspectives. This can lead to more informed and well-rounded decisions. By regularly reflecting on our experiences and asking ourselves questions, examples of which have been provided in checklists at the end of each chapter in this book, we can identify areas within our selves that offer scope for growth and development. This can help us transform ourselves and excel.

The Beginning: Cell to Cosmos

In the current landscape, our society is marred by a multitude of alarming issues that demand our attention and contemplation.

Firstly, violent crimes have become a distressing reality:

- New Delhi, the national capital of India, was once again shocked after the brutal murder of a 26-year-old woman who was chopped into 35 pieces by her live-in partner after he allegedly strangled her to death. Both met each other through a dating app in 2018. The couple started living together after a few days of dating, and her parents did not support her decision. The couple shifted to Delhi in May 2022, where their relationship got tense and they started fighting with each other. He allegedly strangled the victim to death at their residence on May 18, 2022, then chopped her body up and stored the pieces in their new fridge. From May 20 to June 6, he took out chopped body parts of the victim each night and threw them in nearby deserted areas. He continued living in the same flat even after murdering his girlfriend. How barbaric! How could he spend more than a fortnight with the dead body?

- Gun violence, including incidents involving the children and the public, has been a significant concern in the United States. One person opened fire from a hotel room onto a music festival in Las Vegas, killing 58 people and injuring hundreds. His motivation remains unclear, and the incident was one of the deadliest mass shootings in U. S. history. One of the most well-known tragedies is the 2012 Sandy Hook Elementary School shooting in Newtown, Connecticut, in which 20 children and 6 educators lost their lives. These incidents involve a range of motivations, including personal grievances, mental health issues, radical ideologies, and sometimes a combination of these factors. More Americans died of gun-related injuries in 2021 than in any other year on record, according to the latest available statistics from the Center for Disease Control and Prevention (CDC).

- A young woman in Chennai was sentenced to two life terms a few years ago for her role in the murder of her husband while on honeymoon in the hill station of Munnar in Kerala. The court found that the woman had plotted with her lover and childhood friend and his accomplice to kill her husband. Why didn't she refuse the marriage earlier? If she had done so, she could have escaped the life sentence.

- An 11-year-old girl was molested and raped over several weeks at an apartment complex in Chennai by nearly 20 persons, including a lift operator, an electrician, a plumber, and security guard. The culprits allegedly took the girl to various places in the complex, including the basement, terrace, gym, and common restrooms, to rape her. Several of the accused are over 50 years of age.

- A video of a man throwing a petrol bomb at a tusker near Ooty, after which the helpless elephant ran around in agony, went viral on social media. Earlier, a pregnant elephant was killed using a fruit bomb.

News reports of such brutal murders and heinous acts leave us stunned and questioning the state of humanity. We must confront the underlying causes that lead individuals to commit such atrocities and work towards fostering a more compassionate and empathetic society.

Secondly, the occurrence of sudden deaths among young individuals is a sobering reminder of life's fragility. The loss of promising lives due to various factors is deeply unsettling and should prompt us to prioritise our health and well-being. Additionally, the prevalence of unhealthy individuals has become a growing concern. A 2021 report on non-communicable disease (NCDs) highlighted that the burden of NCDs in India, a country with a population of over 1.3 billion, is huge. NCDs in India contributed to 6.8 million deaths in 2019, which is about 67.6% of overall deaths.

The key findings were:
- High blood pressure, intestinal disorders related to digestion, diabetes, respiratory disorders, neurological disorders, cardiovascular diseases, renal disorders, and cancer are the top chronic diseases among Indians.

- Major risk factors for chronic diseases include air pollution (76%), low physical activity (67%), imbalanced diet (55%), stress (44%), and obesity (24%).
- More than two-thirds of people with such NCDs in India are in the 26–59 age group.
- The likelihood of being afflicted by chronic diseases has been shown to increase after the age of 18 and makes a quantum leap when an individual crosses the age of 35.

While ambling through shopping malls, especially in cinema halls, one cannot help but notice people indulging in bucket-sized snacks. It becomes apparent from observing the crowds that they are characterised by a diverse range of body shapes and sizes. Some individuals struggle with obesity while others appear underweight. This stark contrast highlights the prevalence of malnutrition, a condition arising from imbalances in energy and nutrient intake due to lack of awareness. Under nutrition has various effects, including stunting, wasting, being underweight, and micro nutrient deficiencies. These deficiencies can have detrimental effects on overall health and development, particularly in young individuals. On the other end of the spectrum, being overweight or obese leads to a host of diet-related NCDs. Conditions such as heart disease, diabetes, and cancer are on the rise, highlighting the importance of maintaining a balanced and healthy diet.

Although the USA is a 'developed nation', ironically, Americans are not the healthiest people. Sadly, they suffer from many health problems. It's estimated that six out of every ten Americans suffer from chronic diseases like type-2 diabetes, heart and lung diseases, and cancer due to various factors like poor nutrition, insufficient physical activity, drug abuse, mental health issues, and violent behaviour. The same trend seems to be looming over India's future too. Addressing this issue requires an effort to promote healthy habits, balanced diets, and regular physical activity.

The modern lifestyle is often characterised by hectic schedules, sedentary behaviour, and poor dietary choices; high stress levels, a lack of physical activity, increased screen time, and desk jobs can lead to numerous health problems. The prevalence of fast food, processed foods, and excessive sugar consumption contributes to rising obesity rates and chronic health issues. Stress, anxiety, and depression are becoming more common due to various societal and lifestyle factors. The fast-paced modern lifestyle often leads to insufficient sleep, affecting physical and mental health. Gadgets, AI, media, cinema, and advertisements are double-edged swords. They can be both beneficial and harmful, depending on how we use them. Over reliance on technology can lead to decreased physical activity, social isolation, and mental health issues. There are several small, negligent acts that are rooted in a lack of awareness and could have a detrimental impact on our well-being over time:

- *Bad posture.* One seemingly innocuous habit that can quietly contribute to health issues is poor posture. Slouching or maintaining incorrect posture might feel comfortable in the short term, but over time, it can lead to various musculoskeletal problems. Strain on the neck, shoulders, and back can result in chronic pain and discomfort, affecting overall well-being.

- *Improperly chewing food while eating.* Inadequate chewing can strain the digestive system, making it harder for the body to absorb nutrients from food. This can lead to digestive discomfort, bloating, and potential nutrient deficiencies over time.

- *Poor ventilation in living spaces.* Insufficient airflow can lead to a buildup of indoor air pollutants, including allergens, mould spores, and volatile organic compounds. This can exacerbate respiratory conditions, trigger allergies, and lead to a range of health issues. Poor ventilation can also contribute to high humidity levels, fostering mould growth and potentially causing respiratory problems. Additionally, inadequate ventilation can lead to a less comfortable living environment, potentially impacting mental well-being and overall comfort.

- *Screen time before bed.* Modern technology has introduced a new challenge to our well-being: excessive screen time before bed. The blue light emitted by phones, tablets, and computers can disrupt the body's natural sleep cycle and suppress the production of melatonin, a hormone essential for quality sleep. This disruption can accumulate over time, leading to sleep disturbances and fatigue.

- *Skipping meals.* Irregular eating patterns, often stemming from skipping meals, can have a negative impact on metabolism and energy levels. When meals are missed, the body's blood sugar levels can become unstable, leading to mood swings, irritability, and decreased cognitive function. Over time, this habit could contribute to a host of health issues.

- *Drinking water in large gulps instead of sip-by-sip.* Drinking water too quickly in large quantities can lead to bloating and discomfort. It can also overwhelm the kidneys, potentially reducing their ability to effectively filter waste from the bloodstream. This habit may contribute to electrolyte imbalances and, in extreme cases, could lead to a condition called water intoxication or hyponatremia, which can be dangerous.

- *Not drinking enough water.* Staying properly hydrated might seem simple, but it's an often-underestimated aspect of well-being. Even mild dehydration can impair cognitive function, decrease mood stability, and affect overall health. Consistently neglecting to drink enough water can lead to a range of health problems that extend beyond mere thirst.

- *Ignoring regular exercise.* A sedentary lifestyle is a prevalent issue in our modern world. Neglecting regular physical activity can contribute to weight gain, reduced cardiovascular health, and an increased risk of chronic diseases such as heart disease, diabetes, and hypertension.

- *Not taking breaks.* Modern work culture often encourages continuous productivity without adequate breaks. Over time, this can lead to burnout, decreased productivity, and heightened stress levels.

- *Neglecting flexibility.* Flexibility is often overlooked, but it's an integral part of overall physical well-being. Failing to stretch regularly can lead to reduced flexibility and an increased risk of injuries.

- *Poor dental hygiene.* Neglecting oral hygiene by brushing and flossing irregularly can lead to dental problems like cavities and gum disease. These issues can have broader health implications, as gum disease has been linked to conditions like heart disease and diabetes due to inflammation.

- *Overconsumption of sugary foods.* Regularly consuming sugary foods and drinks can lead to weight gain, tooth decay, and an increased risk of chronic conditions like type-2 diabetes and heart disease. Excess sugar can also affect mood and energy levels.

- *Mindless snacking.* Snacking, especially when done mindlessly, can contribute to overeating and weight gain.

- *Ignoring mental health.* In the pursuit of physical health, mental well-being is sometimes overlooked. Neglecting to address stress, anxiety, or other mental health issues can significantly impact overall quality of life.

- *Keeping mobile phones near one's head while sleeping.* This habit exposes the brain to electromagnetic radiation emitted by the mobile phone, which can disrupt sleep patterns and potentially lead to long-term cognitive effects. Prolonged exposure may increase the risk of neurological disorders and impact overall cognitive function.

- *Avoiding social connections*. Human beings thrive on social connections and avoiding them can lead to feelings of loneliness and isolation.
- *Not getting enough sleep*. Consistently getting less sleep than your body needs can lead to a range of health problems. Chronic sleep deprivation can impair cognitive function, weaken the immune system, and increase the risk of various health conditions.
- *Procrastination*. Chronic procrastination can lead to increased stress levels and decreased productivity and can potentially impact mental health.
- *Neglecting mental stimulation*. Failing to engage in mentally stimulating activities can lead to cognitive decline over time, impacting memory, attention, and problem-solving abilities.
- *Ignoring ergonomics in the workspace*. Poor ergonomic setups in your workspace might not seem significant at first but they can lead to discomfort, pain, and long-term musculoskeletal problems.

These seemingly minor acts can accumulate over time to significantly impact our physical, mental, and emotional health and overall well-being. Studies indicate a significant rise in male infertility, with sperm counts declining by almost 50-60% over the past four decades. The prevalence of Polycystic Ovary Syndrome (PCOS), a common cause of female infertility, has been on the rise. There is evidence suggesting a decline in ovarian reserve in women, impacting fertility. Lifestyle management is of the utmost importance for the present generation due to the significant impact it has on overall health, well-being, and long-term quality of life.

When we genuinely love ourselves, we become attuned to the needs of our body and mind, fostering a deep sense of care and responsibility. Loving ourselves enables us to make conscious choices that prioritise our well-being. We instinctively steer away from harmful behaviours, opting for nourishing foods that support our physical and mental health and healthy lifestyles that enhance our vitality and energy.

Furthermore, this new found self-awareness extends to the environment. Recognising the significance of pollution-free air, we become more mindful of our actions and their impact on the atmosphere. Our commitment to preserving a clean and healthy environment arises from our love for ourselves and a desire to safeguard the well-being of all living beings.

As we cultivate self-mastery through self-discipline, our actions align with our values. We embrace a love for nature and others, transcending the boundaries of human connections to experience a profound appreciation for the natural world. This love guides us to treat Mother Earth with gentleness and respect, acknowledging her as a precious entity that sustains life.

The journey of self-love and self-mastery is an empowering process of transformation. By nurturing ourselves, we unlock the potential to create positive change in the world. As we radiate love and compassion for ourselves and our surroundings, we inspire others to embark on their paths of self-discovery and responsible living.

Every passing second, our miraculous body produces a staggering 25 million new cells. In just 15 seconds, we generate more cells than the entire population of the United States. This constant renewal means that every year, our body is essentially new, offering us the opportunity to alter our destiny at any moment. Celebrating birthdays becomes a profound reminder of this rejuvenating power, as we can revitalise our very being at any stage of life.

Beyond the fixed blueprint of our DNA lies a dynamic layer of control known as epigenetics. This intricate system operates through chemical modifications, acting like bookmarks that modulate how genes are read and utilised in the brain. These 'bookmarks' are not static; rather, they are influenced by experiences and lifestyle choices, shaping neuroplasticity— the brain's remarkable ability to adapt and learn throughout life. This opens doors for personal growth and transformation, suggesting that the brain is never truly set in stone. By embracing positive practices like a healthy diet, regular exercise, stress management, and a growth mindset, we can nudge these epigenetic bookmarks in favourable directions, fostering well-being and potentially unlocking our full potential. From mindful dietary choices to intentional sleep hygiene, even seemingly small lifestyle adjustments can have profound epigenetic consequences, contributing to a healthy brain and a fulfilling life journey. Remember, personal transformation is not bound by age but empowered by our proactive approach to experiences and the choices we make each day. So, take heart in knowing that the power to shape your brain and well-being lies within your reach.

Consider this: every single cell in our human form is inherently programmed for health. An astonishing 120 trillion cells come together to create each person, starting from a single, unicellular zygote. The zygote emerges as the first diploid cell, formed through the beautiful union of male and female gametes—the sperm and the egg. This extraordinary fusion brings forth the embryo, the foundation of our existence.

The sheer potential harboured within each of our cells is awe-inspiring. At any stage of life, we hold the capacity for transformation and growth. It is akin to a form of reverse osmosis—rather than trying to change the vast cosmos, we can begin by changing the cells within our own bodies.

In this vast world, a mere one percent stand out as beacons of goodness, while another one percent harbour only negativity. The remaining 98% exist as neutral individuals, capable of shifting their stances depending on circumstances and opportunities. Within this vast sea of possibilities lies the potential for transformation. Empowered by self-belief, these neutral souls possess the capacity to blossom into thriving and wholesome individuals.

In the grand tapestry of life, as individuals embrace profound well-being, their families bloom with vitality and their children thrive with radiant health. As this symphony of wellness reverberates through the bonds of kinship, the very heart of society begins to pulse with vibrancy. A harmonious dance of wholeness ensues, uniting communities in a seamless embrace of vitality.

And in this cosmic rhythm of flourishing, as each mother cradles her loved ones in the embrace of care, the universe itself breathes a sigh of rejuvenation. With every life glowing with wellness, the very essence of existence becomes infused with resplendent vigour—a celestial ode to health and thriving.

Embracing self-love and self-care is not a selfish act; instead, it is a powerful act of self-mastery. By nurturing our cells, we unlock the potential for a healthier and more fulfilling life. As we become more attuned to our bodies and minds, we lay the groundwork for a brighter future, both for ourselves and for those around us.

Let us marvel at the innate potential within us—the ability to change, to grow, and to embrace new destinies. With each passing moment, we have the opportunity to transform our lives and advance toward speak performance.

So be selfish. Here, selfishness does not mean egomania, but self-mastery through self-awareness and self-discipline.

Checklist of Small but Detrimental Habits that Arise from Self-Neglect	Yes/No
1. I am sedentary and rarely engage in any physical activity.	
2. I have poor sleep habits and often go to bed past midnight.	
3. After dinner, I immediately go to bed without a break.	
4. I frequently stare at screens or chat during meals.	
5. I have a habit of eating with my mouth open.	
6. I seldom pay attention to my breathing patterns.	
7. I gulp down a glass of water in just a few seconds and mostly in a standing position.	
8. I don't hydrate properly.	
9. I usually slouch while sitting or standing.	
10. I don't bother decluttering my spaces.	
11. I often skip breakfast due to a rushed morning routine.	
12. I always seek the opinions of others.	
13. I overindulge in unhealthy foods and drinks.	
14. I often make impulsive purchases without considering my budget.	
15. I seldom take breaks to stretch or recharge during long periods of work.	
16. I often follow the crowd in making choices about food, clothes, cultural beliefs, etc.	
17. I forget to floss or rinse my mouth after meals.	
18. I don't pay attention to the ingredients and expiration dates of food products.	
19. I often forget to express gratitude to others.	
20. I neglect to acknowledge acts of kindness.	
21. I often delay tasks until the last minute.	
22. I tend to be a people pleaser by constantly saying 'yes' even when I'm doubtful.	
23. I catch myself engaging frequently in self-criticism and negative thoughts.	
24. I seldom engage in activities that bring me joy and relaxation.	
25. I tend to dwell on past mistakes or worry about the future.	
26. I rarely practise mindfulness or meditation to quiet my mind.	
27. I am aware that some of my actions are wrong, but I continue to do them anyway.	
28. I spend excessive amounts of time starting at screens without experiencing any productivity.	
29. I forget to reflect on the things I'm grateful for in my life.	
30. I rarely express appreciation to loved ones.	

Checklist of Small but Detrimental Habits that Arise from Self-Neglect	Yes/No
31. I often make impulsive decisions that I later regret.	
32. I rarely address unresolved issues with friends or family.	
33. I often suppress my emotions.	
34. I frequently compare my life to others' highlight reels.	
35. I frequently approach my work with a lack of enthusiasm.	
36. I often neglect to review my own performances or actions.	
37. I am inconsistent in my daily routine.	
38. My living space lacks proper ventilation.	
39. I ignore the urge to pee in the middle of the night and try to go back to sleep.	
40. I am inconsistent in my savings habits.	
41. I am easily persuaded by others, even when I know they are wrong.	
42. I need to improve my personal hygiene habits.	
43. I tend to favour sweet and sour flavours when making food choices.	
44. I spend too much time indoors and don't get enough exposure to sunlight and fresh air.	
45. I tend to get easily provoked by situations.	
46. I struggle with effective communication.	
47. I'm dealing with addiction issues related to smoking and/or drugs.	
48. I often don't follow through with the decisions I make.	
49. My fear of facing fear holds me back.	
50. I am unconcerned about the wastage of food, water, and other resources.	

Habits to which the response is 'yes' are those that should be self-evaluated. After reading further, you can take steps, through consistent self-improvement, to create proper systems to correct these seemingly minor yet impactful habits.

Inner Self-care

'The food is the medicine,
The medicine is the food.'

This adage speaks to the profound impact of adopting a holistic approach to our well-being, wherein the choices we make and the nourishment we embrace intertwine to shape our health. Within this philosophy, the definition of 'food' extends far beyond what we eat for mere sustenance, encompassing the very air we breathe, the life-giving water that sustains us, and the warm embrace of sunlight.

In the wondrous journey of life, the things we give our body and mind are like powerful potions that can heal and empower us. Offering our bodies good, wholesome inputs and keeping everything positive is like giving ourselves the best medicine. These nourishing choices strengthen our body and mind, making us feel energetic and alive.

'As you sow, so shall you reap.' When the inputs are positive, we think positively, we see the world through a bright lens, and it fills our hearts with joy and hope. When our thoughts are positive, our actions follow suit—we find ourselves doing good things, helping others, and spreading kindness.

On the other hand, allowing toxic inputs into our body is like poisoning ourselves from within. Junk food, polluted water, and unhealthy air can weaken us and make us feel unwell. Negative thoughts amass in our minds like dark clouds gathering in the sky. These thoughts bring sadness, anxiety, and uncertainty into our lives.

When our thoughts turn negative, our actions often follow the same path. We might find ourselves being unkind, making poor choices, and hurting ourselves or others. It's like a chain reaction of negativity be getting more negativity.

The insidious pervasiveness of negativity fuelled by toxic inputs may be a potent driver of our world's current decline across diverse sectors, jeopardising

global well-being. The good news is that we have the power to change the course of things. By embracing the harmony of positive inputs, we can create a life filled with joy, love, and fulfilment, spreading the light of positivity to those around us.

The Four Foundation Pillars of a Holistic, High-Quality Life

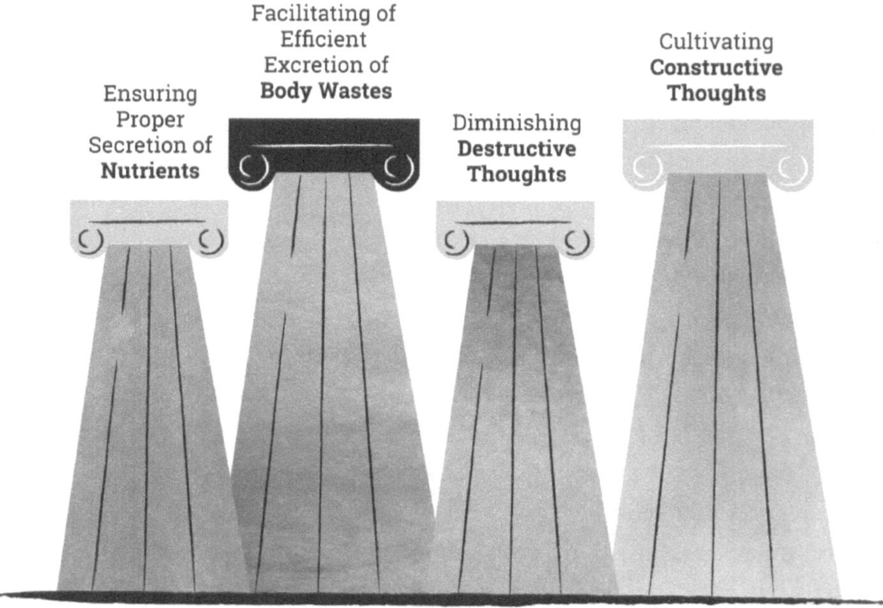

A high-quality holistic life is shaped by four fundamental pillars. Firstly, **ensuring the proper ingestion of nutrients** and minerals is paramount. This entails maintaining a well-rounded and nutritious diet, rich in essential components like vitamins, minerals, proteins, fats, and carbohydrates. These nutrients fuel vital bodily functions, from energy production to immune system support. Secondly, **facilitating the efficient excretion of waste products** is crucial. This involves the coordinated efforts of organs like the kidneys, skin, liver, and intestines to filter and eliminate toxins and metabolic byproducts. Adequate hydration, coupled with a balanced diet and regular exercise, aids in this essential detoxification process.

Moving beyond the physical realm, the third pillar centres on **cultivating constructive thoughts**. This involves developing a positive, growth-oriented mindset. Practices like mindfulness, gratitude, and self-reflection play key roles in fostering resilience, problem-solving abilities, and an overall sense of well-being. Constructive thinking equips individuals with the tools to approach challenges proactively and with optimism. Finally, the fourth pillar entails **diminishing destructive thoughts**. This requires us to recognise and address negative or harmful thought patterns, such as fear, anger, or self-doubt. Techniques like cognitive-behavioural therapy, meditation, and stress management prove instrumental in curbing these destructive tendencies, ultimately promoting mental and emotional well-being.

Through the integration of these four pillars into one's lifestyle, one embarks on a journey towards a balanced and fulfilling life. It's important to note that these pillars are interconnected, and nurturing each aspect contributes to an overall sense of well-being and vitality. Consistency and self-awareness are the linchpins of a holistic approach to health and happiness.

Five Inner Care Elements

Food, water, air, sleep, and thoughts are five integral inner care elements. When we achieve self-mastery in handling these elements through self-awareness and discipline, we can lead a healthy life even in tough times. These five inner elements are interconnected, and, to understand the connections between them, it is crucial to observe our body, thoughts, and feelings, to develop an expertise in our own body language. As we become better at this, we realise that we don't need to be medical experts to grasp the crucial aspects of our own health or comprehend the ailments our bodies may be suffering from. Each body possesses an innate wisdom that surpasses even the vast knowledge of Albert Einstein's brilliant mind.

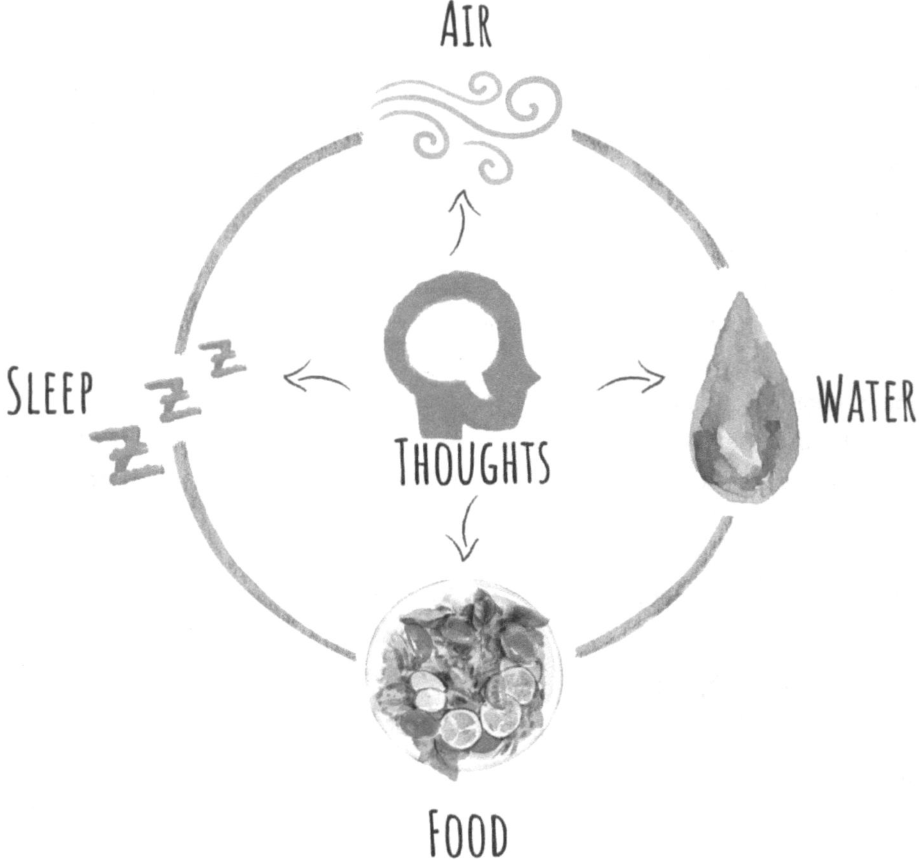

Our bodies are influenced by five mega elements: water, land, heat, air, and space. Water makes up roughly 60% of our body, while the land provides the food we eat. Heat energy keeps our body functioning, and every cell relies on oxygen. The sun is our life source, and even the moon's gravitational force affects us, especially during new moon and full moon days, impacting our mental state.

Food: Nourishment for Body and Mind

Food is the prime source of energy for our bodies, and it should possess not only essential nutrients but also flavour and live energy. Fresh, whole and minimally processed foods contain a vitality or energy that can contribute to overall well-being. Consuming locally grown food is beneficial, as it suits the unique needs of the people who live in that area. Prioritising natural foods like vegetables, fruits, and nuts in our diet ensures a rich supply of live energy and vital nutrients. Sprouted grains are particularly advantageous, as they offer a wealth of nutrients and vitamins.

Gradual Nature of Weight Gain and Importance of Awareness

Weight gain often creeps up on individuals due to its slow and incremental nature. Changes in body weight and shape accumulate over an extended period, sometimes spanning a few years. Consequently, people may not perceive the significance of the issue until it becomes more pronounced. Some may not recognise themselves as overweight, particularly if their environment normalises higher body weight. Fear, anxiety, and discomfort can act as emotional barriers, causing individuals to avoid confronting their weight gain issue. Emotional eating can contribute to weight gain, but people may not fully realise the extent of their emotional eating habits until it has already led to significant weight gain. The link between emotions and eating can be subtle and go unnoticed.

It's crucial to emphasise that awareness and understanding are fundamental in addressing obesity. Regular self-assessments of weight and honest evaluations of lifestyle and eating habits are essential steps in recognising and managing weight gain before it becomes a substantial health concern.

The saying 'drink the food and eat the water' carries a profound truth. It underscores the importance of paying attention to these fundamental activities for our overall well-being. When it comes to eating food, the act of chewing is far more than a mechanical process;it's the initial step in breaking down food into smaller, digestible particles. As we chew, our saliva mixes with food, initiating the chemical breakdown of carbohydrates, fats, and proteins. This well-chewed food is easier for our stomach and intestines to process, allowing for more efficient absorption of vital nutrients, which is essential for overall health. Additionally, thorough chewing helps signal to our brain that we're full, preventing overeating and supporting healthy weight management.

Being self-aware and exercising self-control in food choices are crucial to long-term health and well-being. Self-awareness starts with understanding our own body's nutritional needs. Each person's nutritional requirements may vary based on factors such as age, gender, activity level, and any underlying health conditions. It's essential to be informed about key nutrients like proteins, carbohydrates, healthy fats, vitamins, and minerals that your body needs to function optimally. A balanced diet is the cornerstone of good health. It involves consuming a variety of foods from different food groups in appropriate proportions. Avoid extreme diets or restrictive eating patterns that eliminate entire food groups, as they may lead to nutrient deficiencies in the long run. Self-control in food intake includes monitoring portion sizes. Even healthy foods can become harmful if consumed in excess. Portion control helps prevent overeating.

We have to stay vigilant about reading food labels and understanding the ingredients in processed foods. Avoid items high in added sugars, unhealthy fats (trans fats and excessive saturated fats), and artificial additives.

Eating when genuinely hungry enhances digestive performance. However, when you're hungry and unprepared, you're more likely to opt for convenience foods that may not be beneficial in the long run. The solution is to plan your meal in advance. Practising self-control doesn't mean completely depriving oneself of indulgent foods. It's okay to enjoy treats occasionally, but in moderation. Completely cutting out your favourite foods may lead to cravings and binge-eating tendencies. Staying updated with credible sources of nutrition information will help you make informed choices about your diet. The field of nutrition is continuously evolving, and staying informed can help you make better decisions. It is worth noting, for instance, that adopting a sitting posture with crossed legs while consuming meals improves blood flow to the digestive system, thereby easing digestion and nutrient absorption.

Mindful eating is a practice that involves paying full attention to the experience of eating, including the taste, texture, smell, and appearance of food, as well as the sensations of hunger, fullness, and satisfaction. It involves being fully present in the moment and eating with intention and awareness, rather than being distracted or preoccupied. During the actual act of eating, individuals may focus on the sensations of the food in their mouth, chewing slowly and savouring each bite. It helps with digestion by encouraging the absorption of more nutrients. When we eat, our brains send signals to our digestive system, instructing it to start producing digestive enzymes. When we are distracted while eating, we may end up not chewing our food as thoroughly, resulting in poor absorption of nutrients and incomplete excretion of waste products.

Saliva and Taste: Fascinating Senses

Saliva and taste are essential for proper digestion and nutrient breakdown, nutrient absorption, appetite regulation, oral health, and overall enjoyment of food.

The ability to perceive and enjoy different tastes, such as sweetness, sourness, saltiness, bitterness, and astringency helps us determine the palatability and desirability of various foods. Saliva contains enzymes, such as amylase, lipase, and protease, which aid in the breakdown of carbohydrates, fats, and proteins, respectively. These enzymes begin the digestion process in the mouth, breaking down complex food molecules into simpler forms that can be more easily absorbed into the digestive tract. The act of chewing food stimulates saliva production and sends signals to the brain that help control hunger and satiety. The taste and texture of food also contribute to the feeling of satisfaction after a meal. Saliva contains antibacterial properties and minerals like calcium and phosphate that contribute to the re mineralisation of tooth enamel, protecting against acid erosion and cavities. Humans produce about one to two litres of saliva per day;maintaining optimal saliva production by limiting alcohol/caffeine intake, consuming crunchy and fibrous foods, hydrating, and practising good oral hygiene is essential.

The enjoyment of food and the pleasure derived from taste are important for psychological well-being. The sensory experience of eating can contribute to a positive relationship with food, promote mindful eating practices, and enhance overall satisfaction with meals. The tongue is covered in about 8, 000 taste buds, each containing enormous cells that help us to taste our food. These gustatory calyculi in the tongue convert taste into energy and transmit that energy to all the cells of the body. The sense of taste is not, however, just about detecting the five basic flavours. It also involves the sense of smell. When we eat food, the aromas of the food are also detected by the nose. These aromas are carried to the brain, where they are combined with the signals from the taste buds to create a more complete picture of the flavour of the food. Different tastes are associated with different nutrients. By including a variety of tastes in our diet, we can ensure a more diverse intake of essential vitamins, minerals, antioxidants, and phytochemicals.

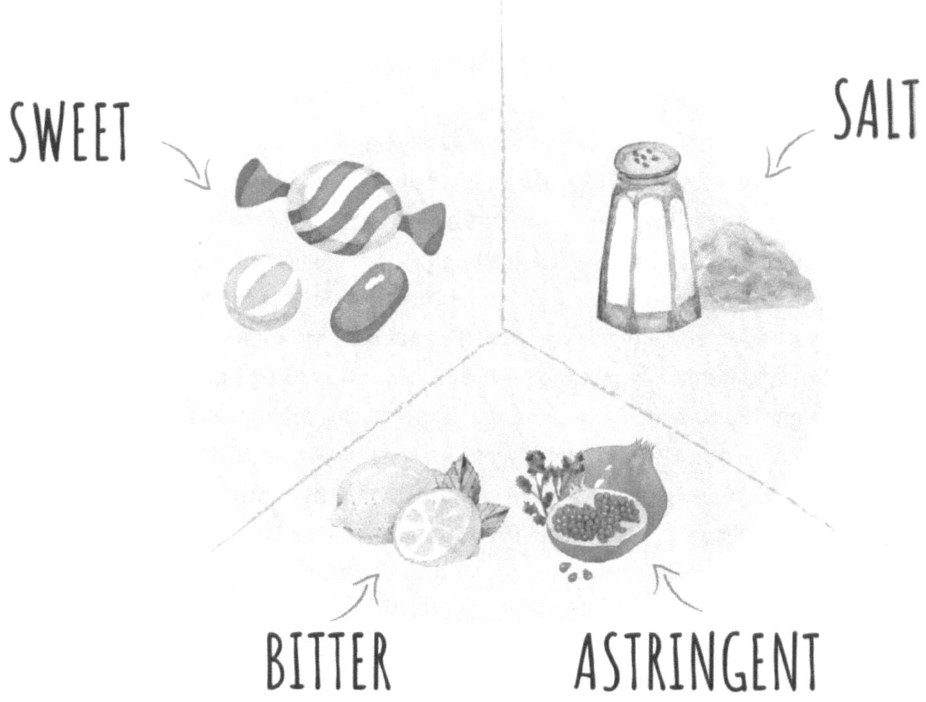

Bitter and astringent tastes, in particular, have important impacts on our food habits and overall health. **Unfortunately, cultures around the world today tend to neglect bitter and astringent tastes in favour of sweet and salty flavours.** This can be attributed to several factors, including the prevalence of processed and sugary foods, the influence of advertising and marketing, and a general preference for instant gratification and palatability.

To maintain a healthy and varied diet, it is important to incorporate a wide range of tastes, including bitter and astringent flavours. This can be achieved by including foods such as dark leafy greens, cruciferous vegetables, and herbs and fruits like pomegranates in our meals. Developing an appreciation for these tastes and diversifying our food choices can contribute to a well-rounded diet that supports our overall health and well-being.

Like Meals, Like Mind

The gut and brain are intricately connected through the gut–brain axis. The gut houses trillions of micro organisms collectively known as the gut microbiome, which plays a vital role in digestion and nutrient absorption. Emerging research suggests that the gut microbiome can influence mood and behaviour through the production of neurotransmitters and other signalling molecules. The brain requires a constant supply of nutrients to function optimally. Nutrients like omega-3 fatty acids, antioxidants, vitamins, and minerals play crucial roles in supporting brain health, cognitive function, and emotional well-being. A balanced diet can improve concentration, memory, and mood regulation. Studies have shown that certain dietary patterns, such as the Mediterranean diet, may have a protective effect against depression and anxiety. Conversely, a diet high in processed foods, sugary snacks, and saturated fats has been linked to an increased risk of developing mental health disorders. Emotions can influence our food choices, leading to emotional eating. Stress, sadness, or boredom may trigger cravings for comfort foods, which are often high in sugar and unhealthy fats. However, this emotional eating can create a negative cycle whereby unhealthy food choices contribute to worsened emotional states. Highly palatable and processed foods can activate the brain's reward pathways, similar to addictive substances. This can lead to overeating and difficulties in maintaining a healthy diet, impacting mental well-being in the long run.

The Rainy Season

During the rainy season, food choices must prioritise safety and hygiene due to heightened microbial growth in humid conditions, the risk of food spoilage in case of power outages, potential water borne diseases from contaminated produce, increased insect activity necessitating food protection, potential scarcity of fresh produce, the importance of cooked food for digestive health, and the need to manage food allergens. Adhering to proper food safety practices and opting for cooked, well-preserved options can help maintain health during this season.

Importance of pH Level

Our pH level plays a crucial role in our body's biological processes. Our bodies have a tightly regulated pH balance, which is necessary for proper cellular functioning, enzyme activity, and other biochemical processes.

The pH scale ranges from 0 to 14, with a pH of 7 being neutral. A pH below 7 is considered acidic, while a pH above 7 is considered alkaline or basic. In the human body, different organs and tissues have different optimal pH levels, and the body has various mechanisms in place to maintain a stable pH balance.

For example, the pH of our stomach is highly acidic (around 1.5 to 3.5), which is necessary for the digestion of food and the activation of digestive enzymes. On the other hand, the pH of our blood is slightly alkaline (around 7.35 to 7.45), and any significant deviation from this range can have serious health consequences.

If our blood becomes too acidic (a condition known as acidosis), it can cause symptoms such as fatigue, confusion, and shortness of breath, and can even result in comas. Acidosis can be caused by a variety of factors, including uncontrolled diabetes, kidney disease, or respiratory failure. Similarly, if the blood becomes too alkaline (a condition known as alkalos is), it can cause symptoms such as muscle-twitching, nausea, and convulsions.

The foods we eat can also have an impact on our body's pH balance. While some foods are naturally acidic or alkaline, our body's digestive system also plays a role in moderating the pH level of the food we consume. For example, citrus fruits like lemons and limes are acidic, but they can have an alkalising effect on the body once they are metabolised. On the other hand, dairy products and meat are considered acidic foods, and consuming too much of them can lead to an acidic environment in the body.

While small amounts of alcohol may not have a significant impact on the pH level of the body, heavy or chronic alcohol consumption can disrupt the body's acid-base balance and lead to a decrease in the pH level of the blood.

While the foods we eat can impact our body's pH balance, the body has robust mechanisms in place to maintain a stable pH balance and keep us healthy.

Food Temptation

Avoiding food temptation, especially when it comes to junk and high-sugar foods, can be challenging but is essential to maintaining a healthy diet.

- Replace junk food in your pantry and refrigerator with healthier alternatives such as fresh fruits, nuts, yoghurt, or cut vegetables. Having these readily available makes it easier to grab a healthy option when hunger strikes.
- Avoid grocery shopping when you're hungry, as you're more likely to make impulsive choices and give in to food temptations.
- Pay attention to your cravings and ask yourself whether you're truly hungry or if it's just a craving. If it's a craving, distract yourself with an activity or drink

a glass of water before giving in to the temptation. Thirst can sometimes be mistaken for hunger or cravings. Drink plenty of water throughout the day to stay hydrated and reduce the likelihood of mistaking thirst for a desire for unhealthy foods.

- Instead of completely cutting out junk or high-sugar foods, set realistic goals to reduce their consumption gradually. This approach is more sustainable and reduces the chances of feeling deprived.

Be aware of situations, emotions, or environments that trigger food temptations. By recognising these triggers, you can develop strategies to effectively cope with them. Tracking your food intake can help you become more aware of your eating patterns and identify times when you might be susceptible to food temptations.

Negative Food Habits

Improper digestion and inadequate nutrient absorption can be attributed to various factors, including the consumption of unhealthy and adulterated foods. Opting for frequent outside meals instead of homemade dishes, eating late at night, and indulging in processed foods further contribute to these issues. Distractions during mealtimes prevent us from concentrating on food while eating it, which hinders proper digestion. Going to bed immediately after dinner and opting for heavy meals at night instead of lighter ones add to the problem. Additionally, consuming water during meals and repeatedly using used cooking oil can have negative effects on digestion and nutrient absorption.

Traditionally, breakfast has been considered the most vital meal of the day, as expressed in the mantra 'breakfast like a king, lunch like a prince, dinner like a pauper.' However, modern lifestyles and a lack of self-awareness have led to a complete reversal of this practice. The importance of a balanced diet and mindful eating is often overlooked, impacting our overall digestive health negatively. Therefore, it is essential to be more conscious of our dietary choices and to adopt healthier eating habits to promote better digestion and nutrient assimilation.

Water: Source of Life for Body and Mind

Water, a fundamental molecule, plays vital roles in biological systems, forming and sustaining life within every human cell. It facilitates the movement of ions, nutrients, and waste, maintains biomolecular structure, and serves as a key component of the cellular cytoplasm. This aqueous environment ensures optimal functioning of organelles and metabolic pathways.

Water is of the utmost importance for a healthy body, since our body is primarily composed of it. While we can survive without food for about 50 days, without water, survival becomes impossible within just a few days.

Proper hydration is essential for optimal brain function, including concentration, focus, and mental clarity. Drinking an adequate amount of water can promote clear and glowing skin by flushing out toxins and improving skin elasticity, can aid in weight management by promoting a feeling of fullness, reducing the likelihood of overeating, and helps lubricate and cushion joints, reducing the risk of joint pain and stiffness. For children, offer hot water after they consume cold items like ice cream to prevent discomfort.

To maintain optimal health, consider the following thumb rules:

- Opt for room-temperature water over chilled water, as it requires less energy to be digested.
- Consume water sip by sip, allowing it to mix with alkaline saliva. This aids digestion.
- Drink water when you feel thirsty, avoiding excess intake to prevent overloading the kidneys.
- Keep in mind that water needs vary from person to person.
- Proper timing for water consumption is crucial:
    - Upon waking up, drink water to rehydrate the body and kick start metabolism.
    - Avoid drinking water during meals to support smooth digestion. Have water at least 15 minutes before or 30 minutes after meals.
    - It's crucial to stay well-hydrated during physical activities. Drink water before, during, and after exercise to replenish lost fluids and maintain performance.

To enhance the benefits of drinking water, consider energising it with the following additions or modifications:

- Fresh mint leaves, rich in minerals.
- A squeeze of lemon.
- Chia seeds (soak them in water for 20-30 minutes).
- Honey for natural sweetness.
- Jeera (cumin), which contains antioxidants, has antimicrobial properties, and aids in detoxification.

It's important to keep in mind that the reverse osmosis process used in RO filters may remove minerals like calcium and magnesium from the water we drink, which, according to the WHO, could have adverse effects on humans.

Air: The Essence of Life

Oxygen isn't just the air we breathe; it's the fuel that powers our very cells! Inside tiny 'powerhouse' structures called mitochondria, oxygen fuels a process called cellular respiration, generating the energy for everything from thinking to fighting infections. But oxygen's impact goes beyond energy. It helps our immune system launch powerful attacks against invaders, allows cells to adapt to low oxygen environments, and even plays a role in cell growth and repair. From head to toe, oxygen's influence is everywhere, making it truly essential for the vitality and health of every cell in our body.

Air is indispensable for human survival. Oxygen, found in the air we breathe, is vital for every cell in our body and is supplied efficiently to them by the lungs. **Lung capacity, heart rate, and weight play crucial roles in determining one's life expectancy.** Breathing is a fundamental and automatic process. However, many people may not be aware of how to breathe optimally for better health and well-being.

To optimise the benefits of breathing, these essential thumb rules are to be followed:

- Practise abdominal breathing, allowing the stomach to expand while inhaling and contract while exhaling, promoting efficient oxygen exchange.
- Good posture can facilitate proper breathing. Stand or sit up straight, allowing your lungs to fully expand without restriction.
- Being mindful of your breath can have numerous benefits for your mental and emotional well-being. Focus on your breathing patterns, and try to engage in deep, calming breaths during moments of stress or anxiety.
- Refrain from smoking, as it directly damages the small air sacs (alveoli) in the lungs, jeopardising respiratory health.

The following activities and lifestyle changes can enhance lung capacity:

- Cardiovascular exercises such as walking, jogging, running, cycling, and swimming. These activities strengthen the heart and lungs, improving oxygen uptake and overall lung function.

- Pranayama breathing practices, advocated by experts like Gregor Maehle, T. Krishnamacharya, and others, which strengthen life force and are known to prevent and cure diseases, restore body-mind balance, and harmonise the solar and lunar aspects of our being as well as the left and right brain hemispheres.
- Minimising exposure to air pollutants like second-hand smoke, chemicals, and other environmental toxins, which can compromise lung health.
- Consuming foods that promote lung health, including apples and leafy vegetables, rich in antioxidants and nutrients beneficial for respiratory well-being.

Maintaining healthy lungs is vital for overall well-being, and these practices can contribute significantly to respiratory strength and longevity. Remember, taking care of your lungs today ensures a healthier and more vibrant life tomorrow. Breathing is a simple yet powerful tool that can positively impact your overall health and energy levels.

Sleep: A Vital Body and Mind Recharge

Sleep is a complex and vital physiological process that impacts various aspects of human health, including cellular function. During sleep, the body undergoes crucial repair and maintenance processes at the cellular level. As metabolic activities decrease during sleep, it promotes energy conservation and efficient resource allocation for cellular functions. Sleep is associated with the release of the growth hormone, which plays a role in cellular growth, regeneration, and the synthesis of proteins. Sleep influences the production of immune cells, cytokines, and antibodies. Sleep is closely linked to neuronal plasticity, the brain's ability to reorganise itself. Sleep influences the regulation of various cellular processes, including hormonal balance, glucose metabolism, and inflammation.

Sleep is an essential body function, serving as a space for the body and mind to recharge. A healthy sleep routine fosters concentration, clear thinking, and proper cognitive and behavioural functions. For adults, getting at least seven hours of nightly sleep is crucial for overall well-being. Lack of sleep can lead to cellular damage, and even after just three days without sleep, cells start to die. Moreover, organs like the liver have biological clocks that work best at night, so getting in and out of bed early is the ideal for the promotion of optimal bodily functionality.

Alarm Bells: Sleep Deprivation's Impact on Health

In recent decades, poor lifestyle practices have led to bedtimes being postponed, which has negatively affected sleep quality. Gadgets emit light and radiation that affects the eyes, brain, and sleep patterns. Chronic sleep deprivation can lead to strokes, mental health issues, high blood pressure, and chronic diseases.

Prioritise Quality Sleep

- *Create a relaxing bedtime routine.* Develop a pre-sleep routine that helps signal to your body that it's time to wind down. Activities like reading a book, taking a warm bath, or practising relaxation techniques can be beneficial.

- *Limit exposure to screens before bed.* Avoid using electronic devices with screens (e.g., smartphones, laptops, tablets) at least an hour before bedtime, as the blue light can disrupt melatonin production and interfere with sleep.

- *Create a comfortable sleep environment.* Ensure your bedroom is cool, quiet, and dark. Invest in a comfortable mattress and pillows to promote restful sleep.

- *Avoid heavy meals and caffeine before bed.* Eating large, heavy meals and consuming caffeine close to bedtime can disrupt sleep. Opt for lighter meals and limit caffeine intake in the evening.

- *Limit daytime napping.* If you struggle with night time sleep, try to limit daytime naps to the early afternoon and keep them short.

- *Address stress and anxiety.* Practise stress-reducing techniques, such as meditation, deep breathing exercises, or yoga, to calm your mind before bedtime.

- *Stay active.* Engage in regular physical activity, but avoid intense exercise close to bedtime, as it may interfere with sleep.

- *Limit alcohol and nicotine consumption.* Alcohol and nicotine can disrupt sleep patterns. Avoid consuming them, especially close to bedtime.

- *Manage sleep disorders.* If you suspect you have a sleep disorder like sleep apnoea or restless legs syndrome, seek professional medical evaluation and treatment.

- *Maintain optimal sleeping positions.* Avoid sleeping on the abdomen for extended periods and opt for side sleeping or back sleeping. Sleeping on the left side is beneficial for digestion and can help prevent snoring.

Remember, a good night's sleep is as important as regular exercise and a healthy diet. Prioritising quality sleep contributes to improved overall health and well-being for healthy individuals.

Thoughts: The Key to Inner Health and Success

The brain, as the epicentre of thoughts and emotions, communicates with the entire body, including individual cells, through the intricate web of the nervous system. This communication is facilitated by neurotransmitters—chemical messengers released in response to thoughts or emotional experiences. Travelling through the nervous system, neurotransmitters can impact the function of cells dispersed throughout organs and tissues. At the cellular level, the presence of receptors on cell surfaces plays a pivotal role. These receptors bind with signalling molecules like neurotransmitters and hormones, initiating cellular responses that can vary depending on the cell type. The activation of these receptors can influence the behaviour of individual cells. Thoughts and experiences might induce changes in gene expression through epigenetic mechanisms.

The two Ts—time and thoughts—are precious gifts bestowed upon each one of us equally and naturally. However, only wise and healthy individuals use these gifts to steer their destinies towards joy, peace, and prosperity.

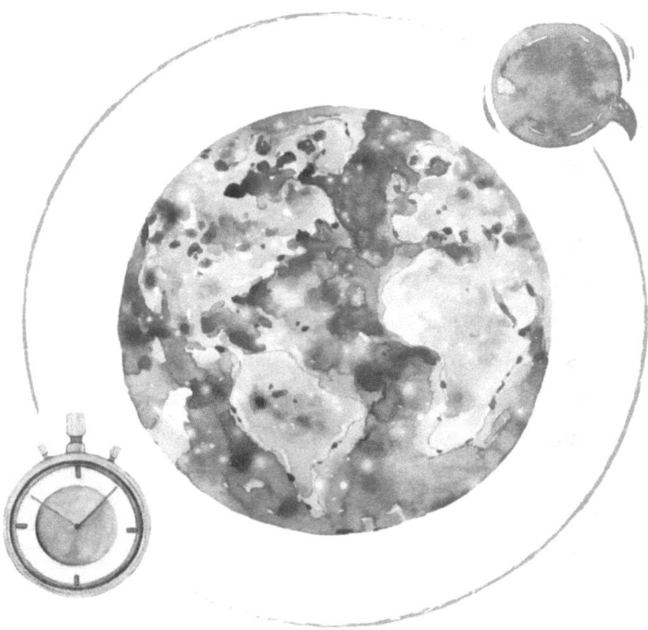

The Profound Impact of Thoughts and Self-Awareness

Thought is the pivotal element among the five inner care mega-elements. Thoughts exert a profound influence on the other elements—food, water, air, and sleep—harmonising them to shape the essence of an individual. The adage 'If you change your thoughts, you can change your destiny' encapsulates the tremendous power of thought. The human brain begins its journey of remembrance even within the womb, and cognitive evolution remains a lifelong process, enabling constant learning throughout our existence.

Our brain, a marvel within the intricate nervous system, orchestrates all bodily functions through a vast network of approximately 100 billion neurons. Astonishingly, it has the capacity to store information equivalent to the entire data run of a TV for 300 years. Although the brain constitutes a mere 2% of body weight, it voraciously consumes nearly 20% of the oxygen supply. However, the oxygen supply to the brain can be curtailed due to factors like stress, depression, overwork, insufficient sleep, and overthinking. This deprivation has a ripple effect on other organs, leading to feelings of exhaustion and demotivation.

The intimate connection between mind and body is profound; each influences the other. Thoughts act as the inner health cabinet, impacting the overall well-being of an individual.

Embracing the power of positive thoughts and self-awareness empowers us to navigate life's journey with clarity and purpose, unlocking the doors to inner health and success.

The Journey from Thoughts to Experience:

'Man is what he thinks all day long.'

- Ralph Waldo Emerson

Thoughts play a significant role in shaping our lives; they are the foundational building blocks that influence every aspect of our lives. They create a powerful chain reaction that shapes our habits and behaviour. Our thoughts are like seeds that we plant in the fertile soil of our minds. They have the power to influence our emotions, state of mind, actions, and experiences.

Thoughts to Experience

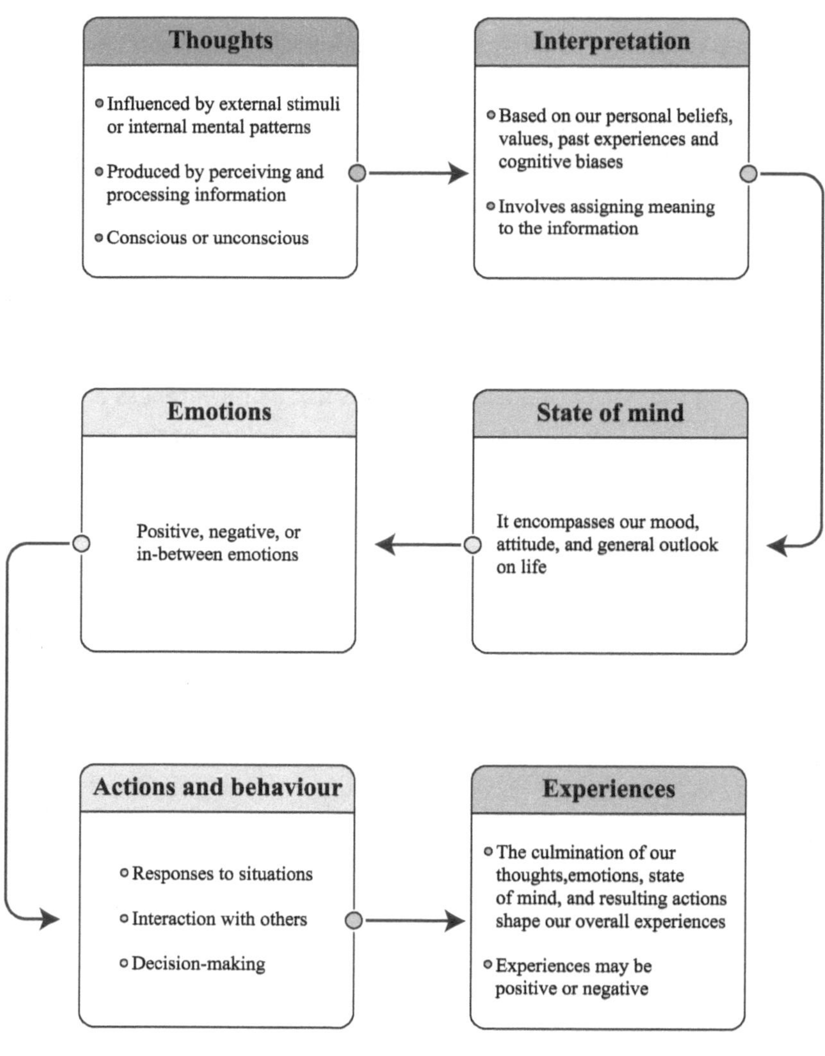

Throughout this intricate process, thoughts serve as the driving force behind our habits and behaviours. By cultivating positive thought patterns, we can foster healthier habits and lead a more fulfilling life. Awareness of our thoughts and their impact empowers us to make conscious choices and shape our journey towards personal growth and well-being.

Strategies to Improve the Quality of Thoughts and Change the Thought Process:
- *Self-awareness.* Self-awareness begins with an appreciation of the intricate complexity of the human body. The human body is a marvel of engineering, with trillions of cells working together seamlessly to support our lives. Understanding this complexity can help us develop a deeper appreciation for our own existence. Each part of our body has a specific purpose. By recognising the functions of our different organs, tissues, and systems, we can gain a better understanding of how our bodies work together to support our daily activities. While humans share many anatomical similarities, there are also subtle variations from person to person. These differences contribute to our unique physical appearances and capabilities. By embracing our individuality, we can celebrate the diversity of the human body. Our

senses play a vital role in our experience of the world. By understanding how our sensory organs work, we can appreciate the richness of our sensory perceptions. Self-awareness also involves recognising the impact of our physical state on our emotions and mental well-being. For example, we know that exercise can boost mood, while relaxation techniques can help reduce stress. By understanding how our bodies and minds are connected, we can make informed choices that promote our overall health and well-being. Finally, self-awareness includes acknowledging the body's remarkable resilience. Our bodies are constantly healing, adapting, and overcoming challenges. Recognising this inherent strength can help us cultivate a sense of gratitude and respect for our bodies. Our thoughts are often accompanied by physical sensations in the body such as stress, tension, relaxation, or discomfort. Paying attention to these sensations can help us identify the thoughts that trigger them and become aware of any recurring patterns or negative self-talk.

- *Mindfulness practices.* Mindfulness practices can help us observe thoughts without judgment and create space for more intentional thinking. Mindfulness is a technique that involves being fully present in the moment and non-judgmentally observing your thoughts.

  - Focus on the present moment: One of the key principles of mindfulness is that we must focus on the present moment rather than dwell on the past or worry about the future. Even if it is a trivial act like taking a bath, paying full attention will produce the desired results.

  - Engage your senses: Another way to practise mindfulness is to engage your senses and pay close attention to the sights, sounds, smells, tastes, and sensations around you. For example, you might take a mindful walk in nature, savour a piece of chocolate slowly, or listen attentively to music without any distractions.

  - Practise meditation: Meditation is a powerful tool for cultivating mindfulness. To get started, find a quiet, comfortable place where you can sit or lie down. Set a timer for 5-10 minutes, then focus your attention on your breath or a mantra, and, when your mind wanders, gently bring it back to your point of focus.

  - Practise mindful breathing: Another simple way to practise mindfulness is to focus on your breath throughout the day. You can do this by taking a few deep breaths and then breathing in and out slowly and deeply, focusing your attention on the sensation of the breath as it enters and leaves your body.

- *Cognitive restructuring.* Challenge negative or irrational thoughts by examining evidence, questioning assumptions, and generating alternative, more balanced perspectives. Replace negative thoughts with positive and realistic ones.
- *Self-compassion.* Treat yourself with kindness and understanding. Replace self-criticism with self-compassion by acknowledging your imperfections and offering yourself support and encouragement.
- *Surround yourself with positive influences.* Engage in activities, read books, listen to podcasts, or spend time with people who inspire and uplift you. Positive influences can help shape your thought processes and outlook on life.
- *Be grateful.* Cultivate a habit of focusing on gratitude. Regularly identify and appreciate the positive aspects of your life, no matter how small. This practice can shift your thinking towards a more positive and optimistic mindset.

Understanding the Nature of the Mind

Understanding the nature of the mind and implementing solutions to address its challenges can help us live happier, more fulfilling lives.

- The mind is susceptible to distractions. In today's fast-paced world, technology, social media, and other stimuli can make it difficult to focus and concentrate. Solutions to this might include setting clear goals, establishing a routine, and minimising distractions by turning off notifications on your phone or computer. It can also be helpful to take regular breaks from technology and social media to give the mind a chance to rest and recharge.
- The mind is constantly thinking and processing information, which can lead to stress and overwhelm. Solutions to this might include mindfulness practices, such as meditation, deep breathing, or yoga, which can help calm the mind and reduce anxiety.
- The mind is capable of growth and change, through the process of **neuroplasticity**. This means that, with intentional practice and effort, the mind can develop new skills, habits, and ways of thinking.
- The mind tends to focus on negatives and can become trapped in negative thought patterns. To address this, it's important to cultivate a positive

mindset, by focusing on gratitude, positive affirmations, and other practices that promote positivity and optimism.

- The mind has a natural tendency to resist change, which can make it difficult to bring positive change to our lives. One solution to this is to focus on developing a growth mindset, which is the belief that our abilities and intelligence can be developed through hard work and dedication. This can help us be more open to change and to see challenges as opportunities for growth and development.

- The mind can be influenced by external factors such as stress, trauma, and negative life experiences, which can impact our mental health and well-being. One solution to this is to practise self-care and to seek professional help if needed. This can include options like therapy, meditation, and exercise.

Impurities of the Mind

Impurities of the mind are negative or harmful thoughts, emotions, and tendencies that can cloud our judgment and lead to unwholesome actions. Recognising and addressing these impurities is often a key aspect of various spiritual and psychological practices aimed at achieving mental clarity, emotional well-being, and personal growth.

- *Negative self-talk.* This refers to the habit of engaging in self-criticism, self-doubt, or negative internal dialogue. It includes thoughts that undermine self-esteem, promote self-judgment, or perpetuate limiting beliefs about oneself.

- *Emotional disturbances.* These impurities involve intense or persistent negative emotions such as fear, jealousy, resentment, or sadness. Emotional disturbances can disrupt mental clarity and lead to unproductive or destructive behaviour.

- *Cognitive biases.* These are systematic patterns of thinking that lead to deviations from rational and objective judgment. Examples include confirmation bias or availability bias.

- *Attachment and clinginess.* This impurity relates to being excessively attached to people, possessions, or outcomes and often involves being unable to let to go of the past, leading to suffering and dissatisfaction.

- *Judgment and criticism.* This involves a tendency to judge and criticise oneself or others harshly. It includes forming negative opinions, making assumptions, and engaging in gossip or unhealthy comparisons.

- *Greed and craving.* These impurities arise from an insatiable desire for material possessions, power, or sensory pleasures. They can lead to dissatisfaction, restlessness, and an unhealthy pursuit of external validation or gratification.
- *Ignorance and delusion.* This refers to a lack of awareness, understanding, or clarity about oneself, others, and the world. It includes distorted perceptions, misinterpretations, or clinging to false beliefs.

To classify these impurities in the mind, you can engage in self-reflection, introspection, and mindfulness practices.

Mastering One's Mindset: Empowering Oneself through Personal Growth

'Mindset' refers to the mental attitudes and beliefs that shape how individuals perceive and respond to various situations and challenges in life. It plays a crucial role in determining one's behaviour, motivation, resilience, and overall success. Recognising and understanding one's current mindset is the first step towards transformation. Mindset significantly influences how individuals cope with challenges and setbacks. A micro-mindset focuses on the smallest and most immediate levels of thinking and action on a day-to-day basis. A macro-mindset takes a broader view to assess such things as long-term financial goals, and a **meta-mindset involves re-evaluating life choices after a major event, as is the case when one undergoes a profound change in one's worldview after extensive introspection.**

Embracing a growth mindset can enhance learning, creativity, and problem-solving abilities. The mindset we adopt can become a self-fulfilling prophecy. If we believe we are capable and competent (growth mindset), we are more likely to put in effort, persevere through challenges, and ultimately achieve success. Conversely, if we believe we are limited in our abilities (fixed mindset), we may not fully invest ourselves in our pursuits, leading to underperformance and confirming our initial beliefs.

Change

- Positive mindset: This involves embracing change as an opportunity for growth, learning, and improvement, opening yourself up to new experiences and challenges, and being adaptable and willing to step out of comfort zones.
- Negative mindset: This involves fearing change, feeling overwhelmed or anxious by the thought of it, preferring stability, and resisting new possibilities.

Success and Failure

- Positive mindset: This involves viewing success as a result of hard work, effort, and learning from failures—a journey rather than an endpoint, requiring persistent pursuit—and embracing failure as a stepping stone towards improvement.

- Negative mindset: This involves fearing failure, avoiding risks to protect self-esteem, believing that success depends solely on innate abilities, and being hesitant to set ambitious goals and limiting one's potential for growth and achievement.

Procrastination

- Positive mindset: This involves acknowledging the harmful effects of procrastination, actively seeking strategies to improve time management and productivity, developing discipline, setting clear goals, and prioritising tasks effectively.

- Negative mindset: This involves succumbing to the habit of delaying tasks and avoiding responsibilities and experiencing increased stress, missed opportunities, and unproductive behaviour.

Overall, a positive mindset involves adopting an optimistic, hopeful outlook towards life, focusing on the good in situations, maintaining an attitude of gratitude, and believing in the ability to overcome challenges. It leads to increased resilience, better mental health, and improved well-being. On the other hand, a negative mindset is characterised by pessimism, self-doubt, and a tendency to focus on the negative aspects of situations. It leads to feelings of hopelessness and anxiety and hinders personal growth. Negative thinking patterns can become self-fulfilling prophecies, reinforcing negative outcomes.

As masters of our mind and emotions, we have the power to tap into our potential by changing our mindset. Though we can't control external distractions and disturbances, we can choose how to respond through self-analysis and self-awareness. **In 1893, Gandhiji didn't allow himself to be provoked when he was thrown out of a railway station in South Africa; rather, he visualised the ordeals faced by Indians in South Africa and used satyagraha as a powerful weapon for change. The rest is the history.** So, instead of blaming others or circumstances, we must take responsibility for our emotions by utilising the gap between external factors and internal responses. By reprogramming our mindset through self-awareness and self-reflection, we can shape our destiny and embrace personal growth, freeing ourselves from societal limitations.

The Synergy of Thought: Embracing Intuitive and Analytical Mindsets

The human brain has two primary thinking systems that are involved in decision-making: the rational system and the emotional system. The rational system, as known as the analytical system or the conscious mind, is responsible for logical, deliberate, and systematic thinking. It processes information slowly and carefully, relying on logic, reason, and evidence to make decisions. This system is located mainly in the prefrontal cortex, which is the front part of the brain that is responsible for executive functions: decision-making, planning, and problem-solving.

The emotional system, also known as the intuitive system or the subconscious mind, is responsible for quick, automatic, and emotional thinking. It processes information rapidly and unconsciously, relying on gut instincts, feelings, and emotions to make decisions. This is located mainly in the limbic system, which is the part of the brain that is responsible for processing emotions, memories, and motivation.

Both thinking systems work together in a complex and dynamic way to influence our decision-making. For example, when faced with a decision, the rational system may weigh the pros and cons, evaluate the evidence, and make a logical choice. However, the emotional system may also play a role by providing gut feelings, intuition, or emotional reactions that can influence the decision.

Ultimately, the interaction between the rational and emotional systems can lead to more informed, balanced, and effective decision-making. By learning to recognise and balance the contributions of both thinking systems, we can make better decisions that reflect both our rational and emotional needs and priorities.

In today's information-rich world, individuals may struggle to strike a balance between intuitive and analytical thinking. Overreliance on one system or the other can lead to cognitive overload and decision fatigue. Under stress or time pressure, individuals may default to one thinking system over the other. This can result in impulsive decisions or excessive overthinking, affecting overall cognitive performance.

The synchronisation of the two primary thinking systems in the human brain is a crucial cognitive process that plays a fundamental role in decision-making, problem-solving, and overall cognitive functioning. Integrating both intuitive and analytical thinking involves a few important steps, but, to begin with, you must become aware of the existence of both intuitive and analytical thinking systems and recognise when each is being employed. Pay attention to your thought and decision-making patterns to identify when you rely on intuition and when you engage in deliberate analysis. **Slower thinking, characterised by deliberate analysis and careful consideration by weighing pros and cons, plays a pivotal role in complex decision-making scenarios.** It minimises errors, enables effective problem-solving, manages risks, facilitates long-term planning, addresses ethical concerns, fosters creativity, supports personal growth, enhances interpersonal relationships, ensures legal compliance, and promotes deep learning. While quick intuition is valuable, deliberate thought is essential for precise and thoughtful decision-making, especially in intricate or high-stakes situations.

Be mindful of cognitive biases that may influence your decision-making. These biases can lead to errors and distortions in thinking. By acknowledging and understanding these biases, you can strive to make more objective and rational decisions. It is essential to cultivate reflective thinking by taking the time to analyse situations, problems, and decisions critically.

- Engaging in discussions and considering different viewpoints can help you gain new insights and challenge your own assumptions by embracing diverse perspectives.
- Trust your intuition when appropriate, but also supplement it with evidence and data whenever possible.
- Combining intuitive hunches with logical reasoning can also lead to more well-rounded decisions.
- Allowing your intuition to spark innovative ideas and then using analytical thinking to refine and develop them lets you explore various possibilities and solutions.
- Integrating lessons from the past can guide your future thinking and decision-making.
- Adapt your thinking style to match the complexity and urgency of the situation at hand.
- Stay open to acquiring new knowledge, skills, and perspectives, as this enriches your cognitive repertoire and enhances your ability to integrate both thinking systems effectively.

When these systems are synchronised and work in harmony, individuals make balanced decisions by combining instinctive responses with logical analysis. They are able to emotionally regulate themselves, as the analytical system can help evaluate emotional responses generated by the intuitive system, leading to better emotional control and decision-making.

Activities such as painting, drawing, playing music, or dancing can help activate the right hemisphere of the brain. These activities encourage you to think outside of the box and use your imagination. Puzzles, crosswords, and games such as sudoku or chess can help activate the left hemisphere of the brain. These activities require logical reasoning, problem-solving, and critical thinking skills.

Regular physical activity and learning a new skill or a new language can activate both hemispheres of the brain, as can mindfulness meditation, which improves focus and concentration, reduces stress and anxiety, and promotes overall brain health. The key is to engage in a variety of activities that challenge and stimulate different areas of the brain to keep it healthy and active.

Understanding the Unconscious and Subconscious Minds: The Perspectives of Freud and Murphy

The term 'subconscious mind' is often used interchangeably with the term 'unconscious mind', but it can also have a slightly different connotation depending on the context. In modern psychology, the concept of the subconscious mind has been extended to include various automatic and involuntary mental processes, such as habits, implicit biases, and automatic skills. It is believed that the subconscious mind plays a significant role in shaping our beliefs and attitudes, even though we might not be consciously aware of it.

Sigmund Freud was an influential figure in psychology and the founder of psychoanalysis. He introduced the concept of the unconscious mind as part of his theory of the human psyche, which was based on the idea that the mind is divided into three main components: the conscious mind, the preconscious mind, and the unconscious mind.

According to Freud's theory, the unconscious mind consists of thoughts, memories, desires, and emotions that are repressed or hidden from conscious awareness. These hidden contents of the mind, often shaped by early childhood experiences and instincts, can have a profound impact on our behaviour and personality. Freud believed that exploring and understanding the unconscious mind could lead to insights into the root causes of psychological issues and help individuals achieve personal growth and healing.

Joseph Murphy, a prominent author and lecturer in the fields of New Thought and self-help, wrote extensively about the power of the subconscious mind. Unlike Freud's psychoanalytic perspective, Murphy's approach is more focused on the practical application of the subconscious mind's potential to improve one's life.

In Murphy's teachings, the subconscious mind is seen as a powerful force that can influence our thoughts, beliefs, and behaviours. He emphasised the idea that the subconscious mind is always active, even when we are not consciously aware of it, and it plays a crucial role in shaping our experiences and attracting circumstances into our lives. Murphy's work often revolves around the concept of 'positive thinking' and using affirmations or visualisation techniques to reprogramme the subconscious mind for success and personal development.

The main difference between Sigmund Freud's unconscious mind and Joseph Murphy's subconscious mind lies in their perspectives and applications. Freud's unconscious mind is part of a comprehensive psychoanalytic theory that aims to understand and address psychological issues through analysis and therapy. On the other hand, Murphy's subconscious mind is presented as a powerful tool for self-improvement and achieving goals by harnessing its potential through positive thinking and mental programming techniques.

'Until you make the unconscious conscious,
It will direct your life and you will call it fate.'

– Carl Jung

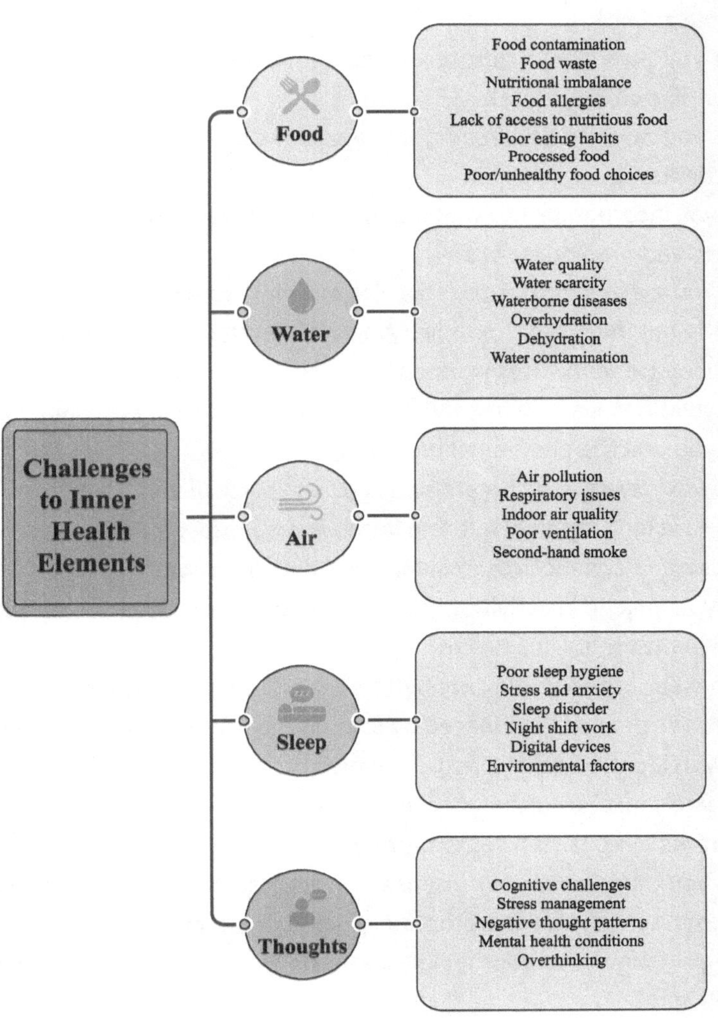

Checklist for Inner Self-care

- Are you aware of how seemingly little things in your life can have a significant impact, either positively or negatively?
- Are you aware that the main cause of emotional issues and negative thought patterns is ignorance?
- Do you eat mindfully, chewing your food thoroughly and savouring each bite?
- Do you eat balanced meals with a variety of fruits, vegetables, proteins, and whole grains?
- Are you aware that consuming fruits immediately after a meal may delay your digestion process?
- Are you aware that deep-frying vegetables causes them to lose their vital nutrients?
- Do you incorporate into your diet foods that cover all five tastes and probiotic foods and prebiotic foods?
- Do you make an effort to recognise each ingredient in your meal, including subtle but important items like ginger and turmeric, while eating?
- Do you experience digestive discomfort, bloating, or irregular bowel movements?
- Do you drink water when thirsty and practise mindful sipping?
- Do you practise abdominal breathing?
- Are you aware that breathing exercises, particularly pranayama, not only increase lung capacity but also improve respiratory muscle strength, reduce stress, and enhance gas exchange and detoxification?
- Do you engage in activities that benefit your brain, eyes, lungs, heart, neck, and joints for holistic health?
- Do you prioritise getting enough sleep and is your sleep restful?
- Are your thoughts influenced by cognitive distortions or generalisations?
- Do you identify and challenge negative thoughts?
- Do you make an attempt to progressively reshape your habitual thought patterns by consistently monitoring your thoughts?
- Do you nurture all your senses, including interoception (awareness of internal sensations) and proprioception (body awareness)?
- Are you mindful of your feelings, especially during moments of sorrow and joy?
- Do you listen to your inner voice?

- Do you regularly express gratitude for the positive aspects of your life?
- Do you engage in creative activities that allow for emotional expression?
- Do you practise conscious presence and mindfulness meditation to enhance self-awareness?
- Do you embrace curiosity?
- Do you maintain healthy boundaries in relationships?
- Do you allow yourself to rest and relax, setting aside time for leisure and hobbies?
- Do you seek opportunities for personal growth and learning?
- Do you spend time outdoors, connecting with nature?
- Do you maintain a journal to reflect on your thoughts, feelings, and experiences?
- Are you challenging your negative or irrational thoughts for cognitive restructuring?
- Did you replace self-criticism with self-compassion by acknowledging your imperfections and understanding your capabilities?
- Do you identify persistent negative emotions or tendencies like jealousy, susceptibility to sudden provocation, or cravings?
- Do you identify your cognitive biases?
- Do you understand how thoughts become experiences?
- Do you know that everyone has the power to tap into their potential by changing their mindset?
- Do you understand your current mindset—whether it is a micro-, macro-, or meta-mindset?
- Do you embrace a positive mindset towards change and success/failure?
- Do you engage in a variety of activities like puzzles to stimulate different areas of your brain?
- Do you pay attention to your thought patterns during decision-making and monitor whether you are relying on your intuition or your analytical thinking system?
- Do you know that slower thinking plays a pivotal role in complex decision-making scenarios?
- Do you know of the ability of the mind to grow and change until death through the process of neuroplasticity?

Checklist for Self-discipline Activities

- Do you create a systematic schedule for self-care, work, and relaxation?
- Do you keep promises made to yourself?
- Do you actively set objectives and prioritise tasks to guide your daily decision-making, particularly when faced with internal conflicts between the two parts of your brain (for instance, when it comes to waking up early)?
- Do you practise intermittent or regular fasting or fasting during festivals to promote self-control and stay healthy?
- Do you avoid snacking excessively before meals to maintain optimal health?
- Do you manage your portions during meals so as to fill up not more than 80% of your stomach, thereby avoid overeating and enabling better digestion?
- Do you limit your intake of unhealthy processed foods?
- Are you aware that having an early dinner can mitigate various health issues?
- Do you identify and address procrastination tendencies to improve your productivity?
- Are you mindful of overthinking and do you practise techniques to manage it?
- Do you set aside designated times to disconnect from digital screens (digital fasting), as social media platforms bombard us with more information than our brains can process?
- Do you keep mobile devices away during the night and turn off network connectivity?
- Are you able to spend at least 15 minutes alone every day to improve your self-awareness?
- Do you put aside one to two hours daily (daily platinum hours)for deep and focused work without distractions?
- Do you avoid overexertion and follow a balanced exercise routine?
- Do you avoid the use of harmful substances, such as alcohol, tobacco, and recreational drugs?
- Are you aware of the overall impact of using such harmful substances?
- Do you consciously refrain from breaking your routines (for instance, by unnecessarily avoiding exercise)?
- Are you conscious of the words you use and do you strive to use positive language?
- Do you follow the anger principle, expressing anger constructively and only at appropriate times?

- Do you cultivate contentment and avoid excessive greed in various aspects of life?
- Do you shop mindfully and avoid impulsive buying?
- Do you track your progress using tools like apps?
- Do you uphold ethical behaviour and follow rules even when no one is watching?
- Do you maintain good personal hygiene by washing your hands and showering regularly and brushing your teeth before bed?
- Do you declutter your space by following the Japanese 5S method?
- Do you refrain from spoiling the environment with waste generated at home?
- Do you refrain from gossip, blaming others, and holding onto grudges?
- Do you maintain the cleanliness of public places, including mass transport systems?
- Do you consider yourself a frugal person, and are you knowledgeable about leading a frugal lifestyle?
- Are you aware that the details of your goals, relationship issues, wealth, etc, don't need to be shared with others?

Physical and Emotional Health

Present You	Future You
is the outcome of	will be the outcome of
what and how you eat,	what and how you are going to eat,
what and how you inhale,	what and how you are going to inhale,
what and how you drink,	what and how you are going to drink,
what and how you think,	what and how you are going to think,
how you sleep, and	how you are going to sleep, and
how you move your body.	how you are going to move your body.

The metaphor of human potential being like a dormant volcano suggests that every individual has immense, untapped capabilities that lie dormant within them, waiting to be unleashed. Like a volcano that lies dormant for many years, human potential can remain largely unfulfilled if not properly nurtured and activated.

Just as a dormant volcano has the potential to erupt and release a tremendous amount of energy, humans have the potential to achieve great things, to create, innovate, and make a significant impact on the world. However, this potential often goes unrealised because individuals may suffer from poor physical and emotional health and inadequate self-care. Furthermore, like a volcano, the potential within humans can be triggered by external forces or circumstances. For instance, a person may be inspired by a mentor, have a life-changing experience, or face a challenge that requires them to tap into their full potential. When the right conditions are met, human potential can be unleashed, leading to extraordinary achievements and personal growth.

In order to fully realise our potential, we need to identify our strengths, interests, and passions, and work towards developing them to become healthy individuals. This may require stepping out of our comfort zones, taking calculated risks, and embracing failure as an opportunity to learn and grow. With effort and determination, we can awaken our dormant potential and achieve great things, just like a dormant volcano can erupt and unleash its immense power.

Unlocking Success: The Power of Systems, Processes, and Routines in Achieving Personal and Emotional Well-being

Having a goal is essential for personal and professional growth and achievement. It provides direction, focus and purpose, helps prioritise tasks, increases motivation, helps with decision-making, provides a sense of accomplishment, and increases resilience. **The main qualities that are lacking in people who fail to achieve their goals are clarity, motivation, realistic expectations, planning, accountability, and resilience.**

Systems, processes, and routines form a crucial trifecta in the pursuit of achieving goals, especially in the realm of physical and emotional well-being.

- Systems refer to the tools, technologies, and resources that help you accomplish your goals. Systems provide the larger framework for how things work together. They are the strategies and methods that guide your actions towards your goal. Many individuals may not be fully aware of the importance of having structured systems in place to support their physical and emotional well-being. The prevalence of digital environments can lead to constant distractions, making it difficult to establish and maintain consistent health systems. The abundance of health information online can be overwhelming, leading to confusion about what systems to follow or what advice to trust.

- Processes are the series of steps that you take to achieve a specific outcome. They provide a clear and consistent framework, i.e. a clear roadmap for how work should be done. Setting unrealistic expectations for immediate results from health processes can lead to frustration and discouragement. The culture of instant gratification can discourage individuals from adopting long-term health processes that require patience and consistent effort. The popularity of quick-fix diets and health trends may lead to unsustainable processes that do not promote lasting health benefits.

- Routines are the habits and practices that you follow on a regular basis. They are the daily or weekly actions that you take to move closer to your goals. Poor time management skills can interfere with the ability to allocate time for essential health routines and self-care activities. Irregular sleep patterns can disrupt daily routines and negatively impact physical and emotional health. Modern work culture can lead to an imbalance between work and personal life, making it challenging to establish and maintain consistent health routines. Social influences and peer pressure can affect individuals' choices, making it difficult to maintain healthy routines when they conflict with others' behaviours. Unhealthy coping mechanisms, such as excessive alcohol or substance use, can interfere with establishing positive routines for emotional well-being. Emotional triggers and stressors can disrupt routines, leading to inconsistency in maintaining healthy habits.

To embark on the path of becoming physically and emotionally healthy individuals, it is essential to raise our awareness about the manifold benefits that proper systems, processes, and routines can bring to our overall well-being. Implementing changes gradually allows us to adapt to new habits effectively, while addressing procrastination and resistance to change by setting achievable goals and celebrating every step of progress propels us forward. Embracing variety in our routines prevents monotony, making the journey enjoyable and sustainable. Practising self-compassion during setbacks or challenges and acknowledging that progress is not always linear nurture resilience. Maintaining a positive mindset and being patient with ourselves throughout the journey are crucial to achieving improved physical and emotional health.

According to the World Health Organization, health is a state of complete physical, mental, and social well-being and not merely the absence of disease or infirmity. This is a holistic approach in which physical-mental health plays a primary pivotal role. The phrase 'sound mind in a sound body' emphasises the importance of the connection between mental and physical well-being. It implies that a healthy body is necessary for a healthy mind and vice versa. This phrase can be traced back to ancient Roman times, when the poet Juvenal coined it in Latin:'Mens sana in corpore sano.' The idea was popularised as part of the ancient Greek ideal of a balanced and harmonious life. It is crucial to promote both physical and mental well-being while recognising the unique challenges and complexities associated with mental health.

Physical Health

Physical activity is required for the proper absorption of nutrients and the excretion of waste generated in the body. Physical activity increases blood flow and oxygen delivery throughout the body's cells, including to the organs responsible for nutrient absorption and waste removal. This improved circulation helps these organs function more efficiently and effectively. It can increase the metabolic rate, which can help the body process nutrients more efficiently and eliminate waste more effectively. Regular physical activity can help improve digestion and absorption of nutrients from the food we eat. This can also help prevent constipation and improve bowel function, aiding in the removal of waste products. Moving the body is the only way to mobilise lymphatic fluid, which strengthens the immune system. The lymphatic system is also responsible for removing waste and toxins from the body.

In a nutshell, regular physical activity helps maintain a healthy body, increase one's fitness level, and improve the immune system.

The Significance of Flexibility

Maintaining flexibility in the body is just as crucial as engaging in regular exercise. Flexibility offers a multitude of benefits that contribute to our overall health and well-being.

- It enhances our range of motion, allowing us to move our limbs and body freely without discomfort or restrictions.
- It reduces the risk of injuries, as our muscles and joints are better equipped to adapt to physical stresses and movements.
- It supports proper posture, alleviates chronic aches and pains, and improves circulation by promoting better blood flow to muscles.
- Flexibility exercises often incorporate relaxation techniques, which help reduce stress levels and enhance mental well-being.
- For athletes, flexibility is indispensable for better performance, agility, and coordination. Moreover, it aids in achieving improved balance, preventing muscular imbalances, and ensuring optimal muscle function.

In sum, flexibility training, through activities like stretching, yoga, or Pilates, complements regular exercise by preparing our body for various physical activities and reducing the risk of injuries, ultimately promoting overall health and fitness.

Essential Steps for a Safe and Effective Workout

Certain common steps should be followed to ensure that workouts are safe and effective.

1. The process typically begins with a warm-up, involving light aerobic movements to increase blood flow and prepare the body for exercise.
2. Following the warm-up, dynamic stretching helps to improve flexibility and mobility by mimicking the upcoming movements.
3. Next comes the main activity, which could be weightlifting, running, swimming, or any chosen exercise.
4. After completing the main activity, it is important to perform a cool-down phase, gradually reducing the intensity of the exercise and incorporating static stretches to enhance flexibility and reduce muscle tension.

Staying hydrated throughout the activity and paying attention to breathing and proper form are crucial for optimal performance and injury prevention. Listening to the body and adjusting intensity as needed is also essential.

Common Mistakes Associated with Different Types of Physical Activities

There are many types of physical activities that can help maintain good health, improve fitness, and increase immunity levels, and each comes with a set of common mistakes that should be avoided to ensure that they do not cause injury.

Aerobic Exercise

This type of exercise includes activities that increase heart rate and breathing, such as brisk walking, running, cycling, swimming, or dancing. Aerobic exercise can help improve cardiovascular health, increase endurance, and boost immunity. Common mistakes in this category include:

- *Starting too fast/too hard*. It's important to start slowly and gradually increase the intensity of your workout to avoid injury and burnout.
- *Neglecting strength training*. While aerobic exercise is important for cardiovascular health, it's also important to incorporate strength training to improve muscle tone and prevent injury.
- *Not maintaining proper form*. Proper form is essential to preventing injury and getting the most out of your workout. This includes maintaining good posture, using a full range of motion, and avoiding overextension or hyperextension of joints.

Strength Training

This type of exercise involves using weights or resistance to build strength and muscle mass. Strength training can help improve bone density, reduce the risk of injury, and improve overall fitness levels. Common mistakes in this category includes:

- *Not warming up.* Warming up before strength training is important for the prevention of injury and improvement of performance. This can include stretching, dynamic movements, or a light cardio warm-up.
- *Using too much weight.* Using too much weight can lead to injury and reduce the effectiveness of your workout. It's important to use a weight that challenges you but allows you to maintain proper form.
- *Neglecting other muscle groups.* It's important to work all major muscle groups to avoid muscle imbalances and reduce the risk of injury.

Flexibility and Stretching

Activities that improve flexibility and stretching, such as yoga, can help improve range of motion, reduce muscle tension, and improve overall physical function. Common mistakes in this category include:

- *Not warming up.* As with strength training, warming up before flexibility and stretching activities helps prevent injury and improve results. This can take the form of dynamic stretching or a light cardio warm-up.
- *Overstretching.* Overstretching can lead to injury and reduce the effectiveness of your workout. It's important to stretch to the point of mild discomfort but not pain.
- *Neglecting to hold stretches.* To maximise flexibility and range-of-motion gains, holding stretches for at least 30 seconds is essential.

High-intensity Interval Training (HIIT)

This type of exercise involves alternating periods of high-intensity activity with periods of rest or low-intensity activity. HIIT can help improve cardiovascular fitness, boost metabolism, and enhance immune function. Common mistakes in this category include:

- *Doing too much too soon.* HIIT can be very intense, and it's important to gradually build up your endurance before increasing the intensity of your workout.
- *Not maintaining proper form.* Proper form is essential to preventing injury and getting the most out of your workout.

Not taking adequate rest. Rest periods are important in HIIT to allow your body to recover and avoid burnout. It's important to balance the intensity of the workout with adequate rest.

Outdoor Activities

Engaging in outdoor activities such as games, hiking, cycling, or gardening can provide a range of physical and mental health benefits, including improved cardiovascular fitness, reduced stress, and increased exposure to sunlight, which can boost vitamin D levels and improve immune function.

Selection of Physical Activity

Choosing the best physical exercise for yourself will depend on a variety of factors, including your current fitness level, health conditions or injuries, and personal preferences. It is essential to choose an activity that aligns with your interests to ensure long-term adherence and enjoyment. Some considerations to keep in mind are:

- The type of physical activity should be in line with specific fitness goals. For instance, if someone aims to build muscle strength, they may opt for resistance training, while someone focused on cardiovascular fitness may choose activities like running or cycling.

- Individual health conditions and physical limitations need to be taken into account. It is essential to consider one's skill level before engaging in advanced or high-impact activities to avoid injuries. Assess your current fitness level. This will help you determine what types of exercises will be appropriate for you. You can start with basic exercises and gradually increase the intensity and duration as your fitness level improves.

- Engaging in a variety of physical activities helps target different muscle groups, prevent overuse injuries, and maintain interest. But some combinations of activities may prove unsafe or ineffective when performed simultaneously. Overlapping muscle groups in a single session can lead to over training and injury risks, while combining intense cardiovascular exercises with heavy strength training might hinder muscle recovery and limit the effectiveness of both workouts.

- Engaging in group-based physical activities or activities with friends can ensure access to social support, motivation, shared accountability and reduced stress. The type of physical activity should be appropriate for your age, taking into account any life-stage-related factors.

Some of the best forms of exercise are as follows:

- *Yoga*. Yoga is a mind-body practice that originated in India and involves physical postures, breathing exercises, and meditation. It improves flexibility, strength, balance, and mental well-being. Yoga mudras are hand gestures or positions that are used in yoga and meditation practices and are believed to promote energy and vitality in the body.
- *Sun salutation*. Sun salutation is a sequence of yoga poses often performed at the beginning of a yoga session. It improves flexibility, strength, and cardiovascular health.
- *Tai Chi*. Tai Chi is a Chinese martial art that involves slow, flowing movements and deep breathing. It improves balance, flexibility, and mental well-being.
- *Qigong*. Qigong is a Chinese practice that combines physical movements, breathing techniques, and meditation. It improves flexibility, balance, and mental well-being.
- *Pilates*. Pilates is a form of exercise that focuses on building core strength and improving posture. It involves controlled movements and breathing techniques and improves flexibility, strength, and balance.
- *CrossFit*. CrossFit is a fitness programme that incorporates a variety of exercises, including strength training, HIIT, and gymnastics. It improves overall fitness and can be customised to individual goals and fitness levels.

The common phenomenon of people starting to exercise with enthusiasm but eventually quitting can be attributed to several critical factors:

- Lack of consistency in maintaining a regular routine and unrealistic expectations of quick results often lead to disappointment and loss of motivation.
- The absence of clear and achievable fitness goals can leave individuals directionless in their exercise journey.
- Overtraining or injuries can further dampen their resolve to continue, while boredom and a lack of variety may make the experience monotonous and unenjoyable.
- A lack of social support and time constraints due to work or family commitments can also contribute to the problem.
- Negative self-talk and mental barriers can hinder progress.

To combat these challenges, individuals should set realistic goals, find activities they genuinely enjoy, seek social support, maintain a consistent schedule, and address any mental obstacles to foster a long-lasting commitment to regular exercise.

Everyone is different, and everybody functions differently. Observe your body using your senses and thoughts and select the physical activities best-suited to its needs. Otherwise, you can consult healthcare professionals. Be sure to start slowly and gradually increase the intensity and duration of your exercise routine as you build your fitness level.

Decoding Exercise Disparities: The Key Role of Personal Determination

Even when individuals share similar age, gender, and body composition, there can be notable disparities in how different individuals respond to and perform different exercises.

- Biomechanics—bone structure and muscle alignment—may grant certain individuals a physical advantage in specific exercises.
- Neuromuscular coordination, influenced by genetics and training, plays a crucial role, but the individual's dedication to refining this coordination is paramount.
- Training history, intensity, and consistency are pivotal; those with extensive experience and rigorous training regimes tend to excel, but it's the individual's commitment and discipline that drive progress.
- The type of exercise chosen by individuals significantly influences their performance. Tailoring one's regimen to align with one's strengths and preferences can yield optimal results.
- Genetic variability affects muscle fibre types, metabolic rates, and athletic potential, yet how one harnesses and maximises one's unique genetic makeup is a personal endeavour.

Taken together, these multifaceted elements underscore the intricate nature of human physiology and emphasise the central role of the individual in shaping their own fitness journey.

Posture

Practising good posture throughout the day, whether sitting, standing, or walking, is indeed crucial to maintaining a healthy body.

- Proper posture helps distribute the body's weight evenly, reducing strain on muscles, ligaments, and joints.
- Proper alignment of the head, neck, and shoulders can alleviate tension headaches and temporomandibular joint pain.
- Good posture allows the lungs to expand fully, enhancing oxygen intake.
- It ensures better blood circulation, which promotes overall cardiovascular health.
- Proper alignment of the spine aids in optimal functioning of the digestive system, preventing issues like acid reflux and constipation.
- Maintaining an upright posture can positively influence how others perceive you, conveying confidence and self-assurance.

Prolonged poor posture can lead to structural changes in the spine and other parts of the body, leading to chronic conditions over time. Poor posture while using electronic devices like mobile phones, tablets, and laptops has become a significant health issue for young people. When using these devices, many individuals tend to adopt a hunched or slouched posture, which can cause a range of health problems.

- It can result in an unnatural curvature of the spine, which can lead to muscle strain, joint pain, and even spinal disc damage over time.
- Poor posture can reduce lung capacity, causing shallow breathing and reduced oxygen intake.
- Slouching can compress the digestive organs, leading to digestive problems and discomfort.
- It can also hinder blood circulation, causing fatigue, numbness, and swelling in the extremities.

A good sitting posture involves keeping your back straight, your feet flat on the ground, and your shoulders relaxed. You should also make sure that your digital screen is at eye level and that you are not hunching forward. When standing, make sure to distribute your weight evenly on both feet and keep your shoulders relaxed. Also, try to avoid standing in the same position for long periods of time and take frequent breaks to stretch and move around. Sleeping on your back or sides is generally best for spinal alignment, but if you are a side sleeper, make sure to use a pillow that is the right thickness to keep your neck in alignment with your spine. Also, avoid sleeping on your stomach, as it can strain your neck and spine.

It is important to remember that being sedentary for long periods of time, whether sitting or standing, can also be detrimental to health. Take frequent breaks and move around throughout the day to promote circulation and prevent stiffness and pain.

Sitting on the floor is a deeply ingrained cultural practice in countries like China, Japan, India, and South Korea. In Korea, for instance, the floor serves as a versatile space for various activities such as sitting, eating, socialising, and even sleeping, like in rural India. This cultural norm has surprising health benefits. Okinawan centenarians, renowned for their exceptional longevity, routinely engage in the act of sitting and rising from the floor numerous times each day. This simple yet effective practice serves as a natural form of exercise, engaging muscles in the legs, back, and core. As they move up and down, their bodies naturally maintain strength, flexibility, and mobility.

The act of sitting on the floor with crossed legs brings about notable improvements in posture. In this position, the body automatically aligns itself, promoting a straightened spine and pushing the shoulders back. This natural posture offers relief from the pain and discomfort often caused by poor posture.

In light of this, it is worth considering the benefits of incorporating floor-sitting into our routines. By embracing this traditional practice, we gain the opportunity to counteract the negative effects of prolonged periods of sedentariness and enhance our posture, increase our flexibility, and improve our overall physical health. Embracing elements of cultures that prioritise floor-sitting may offer valuable insights into maintaining a healthier, more active lifestyle.

Specific exercises can effectively target the muscles that support proper alignment.

- Planks engage the core muscles.
- The bridge pose strengthens the lower back and glutes.
- Wall angels enhance shoulder mobility, and the cat-cow stretch encourages spinal flexibility.
- Rowing exercises target the muscles between the shoulder blades, counteracting rounded shoulders.
- Chin tucks and child's pose promote neck and back relaxation.
- For upper spine mobility, try the thoracic extension and prone cobra.
- Wall chin tucks and scapular retractions aid in maintaining head and shoulder alignment.

These exercises, alongside mindful posture awareness in daily activities, contribute to better spinal alignment and overall posture.

Maintaining good posture during physical activities is crucial for:

- Enhanced effectiveness
- Improved muscle activation
- Spinal health
- Efficient breathing

Poor posture during exercise can be detrimental, leading to:

- Increased risk of injuries
- Reduced exercise effectiveness
- Spinal stress
- Compensatory movements

The Art of Self-Defence Techniques

Self-defence techniques play a pivotal role in promoting personal safety and protecting individuals from physical harm in dangerous situations. Armed with this confidence, individuals can feel more in control of their own security, fostering a sense of empowerment that extends into various aspects of their lives. Moreover, engaging in self-defence training often involves physical activities that improve overall fitness and endurance, contributing to better health and well-being. Beyond physical preparedness, self-defence training also promotes self-awareness and situational mindfulness. Furthermore, mastering self-defence techniques requires discipline and dedication, instilling in practitioners a sense of self-discipline that can positively influence other areas of life.

The first and most fundamental self-defence technique is awareness and avoidance. Being aware of your surroundings, trusting your instincts, and recognising potential threats can help you avoid dangerous situations before they escalate. This proactive approach to self-defence is essential to maintaining personal safety and preventing confrontations.

In close-quarters combat, basic strikes like punches, elbows, and knees prove to be highly effective. These simple yet powerful techniques can be easily learned and applied in high-stress situations, making them valuable tools for self-defence. By utilising these strikes, you can create distance from your attacker or incapacitate them, allowing you to escape safely.

Another versatile and effective technique is the palm heel strike. By using the heel of your palm, you can target an attacker's nose, chin, or throat. This technique requires less precision than a punch and can be effectively employed in close-range encounters.

Knee strikes are also powerful and efficient techniques for self-defence, especially in close-quarters situations. Delivering a knee strike to an attacker's groin, stomach, or head can incapacitate them and create an opportunity to escape.

Different martial arts specialise in different kinds of self-defence:
- Krav Maga is a self-defence system developed by the Israeli army that focuses on practical techniques for real-world situations.
- Brazilian jiu-jitsu is a martial art that focuses on ground fighting and grappling.

- Taekwondo is a Korean martial art that emphasises high, fast kicks, and dynamic footwork.
- Karate is a Japanese martial art that emphasises striking techniques such as punches, kicks, and knee strikes.
- Wing Chun is a Chinese martial art that focuses on close-range combat and using quick, efficient movements to overcome an opponent.

Learning techniques of escaping from common holds and grabs can prove very useful. Wrist grabs, bear hugs, and headlocks are common tactics used by attackers to control their victims physically. Knowing how to escape from these holds empowers you to regain control and protect yourself effectively. Furthermore, knowledge of how to defend yourself against common attacks, such as punches, grabs, and knife threats, should be a part of self-defence training, as should ground defence techniques—real-life altercations may play out on the ground. Knowing how to protect yourself, escape, or immobilise an attacker from this position can be the difference between escaping or succumbing to the attack.

Verbal self-defence should also be an essential aspect of self-defence training. Effective communication can de-escalate potentially violent situations. Learning assertiveness and boundary-setting can help defuse conflicts before they turn physical, providing an alternative means of defence.

Self-defence techniques are indispensable tools for personal safety, empowerment, and physical fitness. Combining physical techniques with situational awareness and de-escalation skills creates a well-rounded approach to self-defence, increasing your overall preparedness and confidence in handling any potential threat. However, it is important to find a reliable instructor and a suitable training programme and to remember that learning these techniques can cause overconfidence and that their effectiveness depends on one's physical limitations and the specific details of real-life scenarios.

Optimal Health of Organs

Each organ in the human body has unique nutritional requirements and benefits from specific constructive physical activities. However, each one can also be negatively affected by certain destructive activities.

Organ	Specific food for the organ	Constructive physical activity	Destructive activity
Eyes	Leafy greens, fish rich in omega-3 fatty acids, nuts, grapes, carrots, eggs	Eye exercises such as focusing on distant objects, blinking rapidly, and eye rolls Eye yoga: yoga poses such as the palming pose or the eagle pose can help improve blood circulation and reduce eye strain Wash eyes in clean water after exposure to dirt 20:20:20 rule: for every 20 minutes of screen time, look at a target 20 feet away for 20 seconds	Prolonged exposure to gadgets, bright screens, or sunlight without protective eyewear Smoking can lead to cataracts
Brain	Fatty fish, nuts and seeds such as walnuts, almonds, and flaxseeds, whole grains like oatmeal and brown rice, berries, dark chocolate	Brain games such as crossword puzzles, Sudoku, or memory games can help improve cognitive function and memory Mindfulness meditation Downward dog pose: this pose can help improve blood flow to the brain Tree pose: this pose can improve balance and focus	Lack of sleep or chronic sleep deprivation Heavy alcohol consumption
Heart	Root vegetables like beets, carrots, sweet potatoes, fruits like papayas, oranges, and berries, vegetables, oatmeal, lean protein, nuts, flaxseeds	Aerobic exercise HIIT Strength training Camel pose Warrior 2 pose	A sedentary lifestyle Lack of physical activity Saturated and trans fats Smoking

Organ	Specific food for the organ	Constructive physical activity	Destructive activity
Lungs	Fruits and vegetables such as berries, oranges and dark leaf greens, whole grains, lean protein (chicken and fish), nuts, turmeric, ginger, pumpkin seeds	Breathing exercises such as pursed lip breathing or diaphragmatic breathing Cardio exercises Cobra pose can help expand the chest and lungs Bow pose can also help expand the chest and lungs (and strengthen the back muscles)	Shallow breathing Smoking and inhaling second-hand smoke Frequent exposure to air pollution and environmental toxins Use of mosquito repellents and coils
Liver	Leafy greens, root vegetables like beets, garlic, ginger, and turmeric, berries, nuts, almonds, chia seeds	Resistance training (e.g. weightlifting) can help improve liver function by reducing fatty deposits Sports such as soccer or basketball that involve high-intensity exercise can also improve liver function by increasing blood flow and reducing fatty deposits	Overuse of certain medications Heavy alcohol consumption
Kidney	Berries, leafy greens, whole grains, nuts and seeds, lean protein, banana stem	Yoga poses (e.g. seated forward bend or child's pose) can improve kidney function by increasing blood flow and reducing stress Swimming is a low-impact form of exercise that can improve kidney function by increasing cardiovascular fitness	Improper methods of water consumption: drinking too little or too much water, drinking water too quickly, drinking a lot of water in one go instead of spacing it out over time Use of certain medications Exposure to environmental toxins

Organ	Specific food for the organ	Constructive physical activity	Destructive activity
Joints	Fatty fish, leafy greens, nuts and seeds, whole grains, lean protein	Low-impact exercises like walking, cycling, swimming, or tai chi	Overuse or misuse of joints can lead to chronic pain and joint damage Lack of physical activity and a sedentary lifestyle can weaken muscles and joints and lead to mobility problems and injuries
Muscle	Lean protein, leafy greens, nuts and seeds, whole grains, low-fat dairy (milk, yoghurt)	Resistance training HIIT Low-impact cardio exercises The chair pose and cobra pose can help strengthen the muscles in the legs, hips, back, and core	Overuse or misuse of muscles can lead to chronic pain and joint damage Lack of physical activity
Teeth	Milk, cheese, leafy greens, walnuts, lean protein, crunchy fruits and vegetables like apples and carrots	Oral hygiene practices such as brushing and flossing Jaw exercises such as clenching and unclenching your teeth or chewing gum can help improve jaw strength and reduce pain and stiffness The triangle pose can stimulate muscles around the jaw and mouth Massaging the gums	Poor oral hygiene practices and a diet high in sugar and acidic foods can cause tooth decay and gum disease Smoking can also increase the risk of gum disease and tooth loss

Organ	Specific food for the organ	Constructive physical activity	Destructive activity
Face	Oranges, whole grains, lean protein, chia seeds, berries, leafy greens, fatty fish	Facial yoga (e.g. lion pose) can help relieve tension in the face Facial exercises Facial massage Swimming Frequent face wash in plain water	Exposure to pollutants Touching the face frequently can transfer bacteria to skin Poor diet Lack of sleep Chronic stress Smoking
Skin	Roots vegetables sweet potatoes and carrots, fatty fish, almonds, pumpkin seeds, tulsi, spinach, citrus fruits	Sun bath in the morning/evening Shoulder stand pose can improve blood flow to the face and skin, as well as stimulate the lymphatic system to remove toxins Fish pose can also improve blood flow to the face and skin and reduce stress, which can improve skin health Swimming Skincare routine: cleansing, moisturising, and protecting your skin from the sun and environmental factors	Poor skincare practices such as not drinking enough water, over-cleansing, and sleeping with makeup on can clog skin pores Using expired skin care products and exposure to environmental toxins can cause damage the skin and cause premature aging Mosquito repellents and coils
Nerves	Brown rice, nuts and seeds, lean protein, leafy greens, low-fat dairy	Stretching exercises Yoga poses such as the child's pose or the corpse pose can help reduce stress and improve nerve function Relaxation techniques such as meditation or deep breathing exercises can help reduce stress and improve overall nerve function Neck exercises	Chronic stress Certain health issues such as multiple sclerosis and Parkinson's disease

Organ	Specific food for the organ	Constructive physical activity	Destructive activity
Blood	Fruits such as berries, oranges, and pomegranates contain antioxidants and flavonoids; leafy greens like tulsi, spinach and kale, as well as beets and garlic, contain nitrates that help improve blood flow; fatty fish like salmon, nuts and seeds, and avocados contain omega-3 fatty acids that help reduce inflammation	Any form of cardio exercises, strength training, and certain yoga poses, such as the downward dog, the cobra pose, or the triangle pose, can improve blood circulation Joint exercises by rotating joints, which produces blood in bone marrow	A sedentary lifestyle can lead to poor blood circulation as it reduces the flow of blood through the veins and arteries Chronic stress can cause the blood vessels to constrict A diet high in saturated fats, cholesterol, and salt can increase the risk of high blood pressure, plaque buildup, and blood vessel damage Excessive use of alcohol Smoking
Spine	Diet rich in nutrients such as calcium, vitamin D, and magnesium, leafy greens, dairy products, nuts and seeds, fatty fish	Regular exercise, yoga, Pilates, and core strengthening exercises Maintaining good posture: when sitting, it's important to keep your back straight and your feet flat on the ground; when standing, make sure to distribute your weight evenly on both feet and keep your shoulders relaxed	Poor posture, particularly while on one's mobile, and sedentary lifestyle increase the risk of developing spine problems Smoking Alcohol consumption Lifting heavy objects improperly

Emotional Health

'Ignorance precedes victimisation,
Victimisation precedes awareness,
Awareness precedes change,
Change precedes challenge,
Challenge precedes excellence.'

Emotions are complex psychological and physiological experiences that involve various bodily responses. When we experience an emotion, our brain sends signals to different parts of our body, which can trigger a range of physiological responses like sweating, changes in heart rate and blood pressure, which are part of the body's fight or flight response, changes in facial expressions, digestive changes, breathing changes, etc.

Emotions and the secretion of hormones in the human body are closely linked to each other, but they are different. Hormones are chemical messengers that are produced by various glands and travel through the bloodstream to target cells or organs, where they regulate various physiological processes. Emotions, on the other hand, are subjective experiences that involve a complex interplay of psychological and physiological processes.

Positive emotions, such as joy, love, and contentment, have been shown to have a number of benefits for our physical and mental health. When we experience positive emotions, the brain releases hormones such as dopamine and serotonin, which promote feelings of pleasure and well-being. These hormones can have a number of positive effects on the body; they reduce inflammation, boost the immune system, and improve cardiovascular function.

On the other hand, negative emotions, such as jealousy, anxiety, hostility, and sadness, can have a number of negative effects on our physical and mental health. When we experience negative emotions, the brain releases stress hormones such as cortisol and adrenaline, which can have harmful effects on the body if they are released too frequently or for too long. Chronic stress and negative emotions have been linked to a number of health problems, including cardiovascular disease, diabetes, and depression.

As discussed earlier, **emotional awareness** is the ability to recognise and understand your own emotions as well as the emotions of others. It is an essential component of mental and emotional health and plays a crucial role in developing healthy relationships and coping with stress and challenges in life. When you're emotionally aware, you have a better understanding of your own feelings, needs, and behaviours. This self-awareness can help you make better decisions, set boundaries, and communicate more effectively with others. Emotional awareness helps you understand the emotions of others, which can improve your communication and relationships. When you can recognise and respond to the emotions of others, you're more likely to communicate in a way that is respectful and effective. Emotional awareness can help you manage stress, anxiety, and depression. When you're aware of your emotions, you're better equipped to cope with negative feelings and find healthy ways to manage them. Emotional awareness can also increase your empathy and compassion for others. When you can recognise and understand the emotions of others, you're more likely to respond with kindness and empathy, which can improve your relationships and overall well-being.

Emotional awareness is a key component of emotional intelligence, which is an important skill for success in both personal and professional lives. Emotional intelligence involves the ability to regulate your own emotions, recognise the emotions of others, and use that information to guide your thoughts and behaviour. Developing emotional awareness takes time and effort, but the benefits are well worth it.

Understanding the Adaptive Role of Fear, Anger, and Stress

Fear, anger, and stress are all natural emotions that serve an important purpose in human survival and well-being. It's important to note, however, that excessive or prolonged fear, anger, and stress can be harmful to our physical and mental health.

Fear helps us respond to potential threats by triggering our 'fight or flight' response. This response prepares our bodies to either confront the danger or flee from it. Without fear, we may not be able to recognise danger and respond appropriately, which could put us in harm's way.

Anger is a natural response to perceived threats, injustices, or violations of our boundaries. It can motivate us to take action to protect ourselves, stand up for our rights, or assert ourselves in challenging situations. Without anger, we may be more likely to accept mistreatment or injustice without fighting back. According to Aristotle, anger should be expressed in a controlled and proportionate manner. He argued that excessive anger or uncontrolled outbursts could lead to violence and harm while repressed anger could lead to depression and other psychological problems. Overall, Aristotle's principle of anger emphasises the importance of channelling anger in a constructive way that promotes justice and social change instead of causing harm or perpetuating injustice.

While chronic stress can be harmful, some amount of stress can actually be beneficial. It can motivate us to take action and perform at our best, improve our cognitive function, and help us adapt to challenging situations. Without any stress, we may become complacent and unmotivated.

So, while these emotions can be useful in certain situations, it's important to learn to manage them effectively to avoid negative impacts.

Intellectual Clarity: Unravelling Cognitive Biases and Distortions

Cognitive biases are inherent flaws in human thinking processes that can lead to deviations from rational decision-making. They can impact our perceptions, judgments, and decisions in various situations. Cognitive distortions, on the other hand, are specific types of biased thinking patterns that are commonly associated with mental health conditions like depression and anxiety. These distortions involve negative and irrational thought patterns, which can exacerbate emotional distress and affect one's perception of reality. Cognitive biases are general thinking tendencies that can affect anyone, while cognitive distortions are specific irrational thinking patterns often associated with certain psychological conditions.

Some of the common cognitive biases and their implications:

- *Confirmation bias.* This bias occurs when we seek, interpret, or remember information in a way that confirms our pre-existing beliefs or hypotheses. It can lead to closed-mindedness and a lack of consideration for alternative viewpoints.
- *Availability heuristic.* This bias involves relying on readily available information or examples that come to mind quickly when making judgments. It can lead to overestimating the likelihood of events that are more easily recalled, regardless of their actual probability.
- *Anchoring bias.* This bias occurs when we rely too heavily on the first piece of information encountered (the 'anchor') when making decisions. Subsequent judgments are then adjusted based on this initial anchor, often leading to inaccurate assessments.

- *Overconfidence bias.* This bias involves overestimating one's abilities, knowledge, or the accuracy of predictions. It can lead to poor decision-making and a failure to adequately consider risks and uncertainties.
- *Hindsight bias.* Also known as the 'I-knew-it-all-along' effect, this bias makes people believe that past events were more predictable than they actually were. It can make it difficult to learn from past mistakes and evaluate decision-making processes objectively.
- *Gambler's fallacy.* This bias occurs when individuals believe that past random events can influence the outcome of future random events. An example of this is the belief that, after a series of coin tosses landing heads, the next toss is more likely to land tails, which is incorrect.
- *Self-serving bias.* This bias involves attributing positive outcomes to internal factors (e.g. abilities or efforts) while blaming negative outcomes on external factors (e.g. luck or others). It can lead to a distorted self-perception and hinder personal growth.
- *Sunk cost fallacy.* This bias occurs when individuals continue investing in a decision or project because they believe they have already invested a lot, even if the prospects for success are low. It can lead to a persistent and irrational commitment to failing endeavours.
- *Bandwagon effect.* This bias involves adopting certain beliefs or behaviours simply because many others are doing so. It can lead to a herd mentality and the uncritical acceptance of ideas without careful consideration.
- *Fundamental attribution error.* This bias involves overemphasising internal factors when explaining others' behaviour while under emphasising situational or external factors. It can cause us to misread people's actions and can subsequently lead to misunderstandings and misjudgements.

Some common types of cognitive distortions:
- *Black-and-white thinking.* Also known as dichotomous thinking or all-or-nothing thinking, this is a cognitive distortion whereby individuals perceive things as being either entirely positive or entirely negative, with no shades of grey or middle ground.
- *Over generalisation.* This distortion occurs when a single negative event is seen as a never-ending pattern of defeat. For example, someone may believe that, because they failed at one task, they will fail at all future tasks as well.

- *Catastrophising*. Catastrophising involves magnifying the impact of a negative event and imagining the worst possible outcome. This can lead to excessive worry and anxiety.
- *Personalisation*. This distortion occurs when individuals take responsibility for events that are beyond their control or not related to them. They may believe that external events are a result of their actions or characteristics.
- *Mind reading*. This distortion involves assuming that we know what others are thinking without concrete evidence. It can lead to misunderstandings and strained relationships.
- *Fortune telling*. This distortion involves predicting negative outcomes with certainty, even when there is no evidence to support such predictions. It can create unnecessary anxiety and prevent individuals from taking positive actions.
- *Emotional reasoning*. This distortion involves assuming that, because we feel a certain way, our emotions must reflect reality. For example, feeling inadequate in a situation and concluding that we must be incompetent, even if the evidence suggests otherwise.
- *Should statements*. 'Should' statements involve imposing rigid and unrealistic expectations on oneself or others. They can lead to feelings of guilt, frustration, and disappointment.
- *Labelling*. Labelling involves assigning global and negative labels to oneself or others based on specific behaviours or mistakes. It can lead to low self-esteem and affect self-worth.
- *Discounting the positive*. This distortion entails dismissing positive experiences or accomplishments, believing that they are insignificant or don't count. It can perpetuate feelings of dissatisfaction and inadequacy.

Steps to be taken to avoid thinking errors:
- *Educate yourself*. Begin by expanding your knowledge. Delve into books, articles, and resources that discuss cognitive biases, logical fallacies, and the art of critical thinking. Gaining a deep understanding of these thinking errors will empower one to identify them within one's thought processes.
- *Develop self-awareness*. Cultivate a heightened level of self-awareness by paying close attention to your own thoughts, emotions, and decision-making. Be mindful of recurring thinking patterns that may be influenced by cognitive biases or irrational thought processes.

- *Question assumptions.* Challenge the very assumptions and beliefs you hold by asking yourself why you embrace certain beliefs, whether these beliefs are grounded in solid evidence or in emotional biases.
- *Seek different perspectives.* Actively pursue diverse viewpoints and opinions to broaden your understanding of a subject. Extend your reach to consider alternative arguments, fostering a more comprehensive view.
- *Delay judgment.* Practise patience in decision-making. Avoid impulsive choices and invest time in gathering information, analysing the situation, and conscientiously evaluating potential biases that may taint judgment.
- *Apply critical thinking.* Engage in critical thinking by assessing evidence meticulously, weighing the pros and cons, and pondering the far-reaching implications of decisions.
- *Test ideas.* Embrace a spirit of experimentation and a readiness to subject ideas and hypotheses to scrutiny. Feedback and trials will refine thinking and decision-making processes.
- *Beware of heuristics.* Stay vigilant regarding mental shortcuts and heuristics that may tempt you into biased judgments. Understand the limitations of these shortcuts and make a conscious effort to overcome them.
- *Learn from mistakes.* Welcome failures as invaluable opportunities for learning. Analyse past errors to uncover cognitive biases that may have contributed to them, ensuring personal growth.
- *Practise reflection.* Make it a habit to periodically reflect on decisions and thought processes. Ponder what transpired well and what could have been handled differently, applying your new found knowledge of cognitive biases to these reflections.

Manifestation in the Mind and Its Background

The constant negative thoughts and images can manifest as anxiety, stress, fear, and even depression. There can be many emotional manifestations in the mind, each of them with psychological or cognitive backgrounds that contribute to them. It's important to remember that these manifestations are not necessarily always accurate or reflective of reality; rather, they are products of one's thoughts, feelings, and beliefs. While some manifestations in the mind might have psychological or cognitive backgrounds, others might be influenced by external factors/life circumstances—financial situation, health, living conditions, relationships, societal pressures, etc. Addressing these manifestations often involves working through the underlying psychological and cognitive processes and making positive changes in one's life.

Manifestation	Possible Background
Believing that you are unworthy of love and relationships	Low self-esteem, past negative experiences in relationships, negative self-talk
Thinking that you are not good enough to succeed in your career	Fear of failure, lack of confidence, comparison to others, societal pressures and expectations
Constantly worrying about the future and what might go wrong	Anxiety, lack of control over the future, past negative experiences, catastrophising
Feeling stuck or stagnant in life and not making progress towards your goals	Lack of motivation, unclear goals, fear of change, limiting beliefs
Attracting negative people or experiences into your life	Negative self-talk, low self-esteem, lack of boundaries, past negative experiences
Avoidance of tasks	Fear of failure, lack of motivation, perfectionism, anxiety
Self-doubt and imposter syndrome	Comparison to others, lack of confidence, fear of failure, societal pressures
Difficulty expressing emotions or setting boundaries	Past negative experiences, fear of rejection, lack of self-awareness, low self-esteem
Negative self-talk or self-criticism	Low self-esteem, past negative experiences, anxiety, depression
Difficulty with decision-making	Fear of making the wrong choice, lack of self-confidence, lack of information or resources, indecisiveness
Attracting negative people or experiences into your life	Negative self-talk, low self-esteem, lack of boundaries, past negative experiences

Psychological Techniques

Psychological techniques can be very useful tools for a variety of reasons. They can help individuals manage difficult emotions, change negative patterns, promote self-awareness, reduce symptoms of mental illness, etc.

These techniques, like mindful walking, mindful breathing, and mindful eating, can help individuals become more aware of their emotional experiences and develop strategies for responding to them in a healthy and productive way.

The body scan is a mindful meditation technique that involves paying attention to physical sensations in different parts of your body. It can be a useful tool for reducing stress, managing pain, and increasing self-awareness. The body scan can be a helpful way to connect with your body, release tension, and cultivate a greater sense of relaxation and self-awareness. You can do this exercise anytime and anywhere, whenever you feel the need to ground yourself and become more present in the moment.

Many psychological techniques, like cognitive behavioural therapy or thought-stopping, are designed to help individuals identify and challenge negative thought patterns. These techniques can help individuals shift their thinking from a negative, self-defeating mindset to a more positive and constructive one.

- Techniques like *dialectical behaviour therapy or emotion-focused therapy* can help individuals improve their communication skills and develop healthier and more satisfying relationships with others.
- Techniques like *journalling or self-reflection exercises* can help individuals develop a greater sense of self-awareness and identify areas for personal growth and development.
- Techniques like *exposure therapy* are often used to treat mental illnesses like anxiety disorders or post-traumatic stress disorder. These techniques can help individuals reduce symptoms of these conditions and improve their overall quality of life.
- *Expressive writing*. This technique involves writing about thoughts and emotions related to a difficult experience on a sheet of paper and tearing it up, with the goal of processing and releasing negative emotions, instead of sharing those feelings with others. It shreds up the ill-feelings generated in the ordeal.
- *Sleep hygiene*. This refers to a set of practices that promote high-quality sleep by creating a relaxing sleep environment, avoiding stimulating activities before bed time, keeping the stomach light before bed, avoiding the consumption of caffeine and alcohol, maintaining the same sleep and wake-up times, etc, all of which will have a positive impact on overall health and well-being.
- *Mind-mapping*. This technique involves creating a visual diagram of ideas or concepts, with the goal of organising and clarifying one's thoughts.
- *Ho'oponopono*. This technique is a Hawaiian practice of reconciliation and forgiveness, which involves repeating phrases like 'I'm sorry', 'thank you',

'please forgive me', and 'I love you' as a way of promoting healing and resolution.

- *Switch words*. This technique involves using specific words or phrases to shift one's mindset or energy in a positive direction.
- *Postponement*. This technique involves intentionally delaying a decision or action in order to give oneself more time to consider options and avoid impulsive or reactive behaviour.
- *Five-second rule*. This technique involves taking action within five seconds of having an idea or impulse, in order to overcome procrastination and make progress towards one's goals.
- *Reverse psychology*. This technique involves using language or behaviour that encourages someone to do the opposite of what is expected or desired, with the goal of achieving a desired outcome indirectly.

It's worth noting that different techniques may be more effective for different individuals and for different situations.

Memory Retention

Memory retention plays a critical role in our daily lives and is essential for learning, problem-solving, communication, safety, sense of personal identity, and mental health. Memory impairment can be a symptom of various neurological and psychiatric conditions, and the ability to remember positive experiences and memories can play a role in promoting mental well-being.

The fundamental components of memory retention are attention, encoding, storage, retrieval, repetition, organising information, elaboration, and contextual cues. Paying attention to the information you want to retain is crucial. When you focus your attention on something, you are more likely to remember it later. Creating associations between new bits of information and existing knowledge can help with elaboration. Contextual cues, such as the environment or emotions present when information is learnt, can help trigger recall.

Some mind retention techniques include:
- *Mind mapping*. As discussed above, mind mapping can help you organise and remember complex information. For example, if you're studying for a history exam, you can create a mind map that organises key events, dates, and people.

- *Active recall.* Active recall is a technique that involves actively recalling information without looking at notes or books. This helps strengthen memory traces and improve recall. For example, after reading a chapter in a book, try to recall the main points without looking back at the chapter.
- *Repetition.* Repetition is a simple but effective technique for retaining information. Repeating information over time helps to strengthen memory traces and makes it easier to recall later. For example, when learning new words, repeat them several times throughout the day to help remember them.
- *Chunking.* Chunking is a technique that involves breaking down large amounts of information into smaller, more manageable chunks. This can make it easier to remember and recall information. For example, when memorising a long phone number, break it down into smaller groups of numbers.
- *Visualisation.* Visualisation involves creating mental images to help remember information. Hyperphantasia is the condition of having highly vivid mental imagery, akin to actual sight. Aphantasia, on the other hand, is the absence of visual images in one's mind. Overcoming aphantasia, the inability to generate mental images, is a personal journey that varies for each individual. One approach involves regular visualisation exercises, starting with simple objects and progressing to more complex scenes. Associating other senses like touch, smell, or sound with concepts may also help trigger mental imagery. It's important to remember that aphantasia is a natural cognitive variation, and finding ways to improve visualisation should be approached with an open mind and without undue pressure.
- *Association.* Association involves creating connections between new information and information that is already familiar. This can help make new information easier to remember. For example, when learning new words, try to associate each word with a familiar object or image.
- *Mnemonics.* Mnemonics are memory aids that use visual or auditory cues to help with information recall. For example, 'My very eager mother just served us nine pizzas', in which the order of the first letters of every word is the same as the order of the first letters of the names of the planets(Mercury, Venus, Earth, Mars, Jupiter, Saturn, Uranus, Neptune, Pluto), was a mnemonic used to remember the order of the planets in our solar system when Pluto was considered a planet.

Memory retention is a critical cognitive process that plays a role in various aspects of our lives, and it is essential for optimal cognitive functioning and well-being.

Auto-suggestion and Hetero-suggestion:

Auto-suggestions can be more important than hetero-suggestions for emotional awakening because they come from within and are based on an individual's own beliefs, experiences, and desires. Emotional awakening often involves a deepening of self-awareness and an increased ability to connect with one's own emotions and feelings. Auto-suggestions can help facilitate this process by allowing individuals to tap into their own inner wisdom and intuition.

Through the use of auto-suggestions, individuals can become more attuned to their own emotions and needs. By regularly affirming positive beliefs and intentions, individuals can shift their mindset and create new neural pathways in the brain that support emotional growth and well-being. This can lead to increased self-awareness, self-confidence, and a greater sense of inner peace and fulfilment.

Hetero-suggestions, on the other hand, may be less effective for emotional awakening because they come from external sources and may not align with an individual's own values or experiences. While feedback and guidance from others can be valuable, ultimately, true emotional awakening must come from within.

In addition, the power of auto-suggestion lies in its ability to tap into the subconscious mind. The subconscious mind, as discussed earlier, is the seat of our beliefs, habits, and emotions, and is often resistant to change. By consistently affirming positive beliefs and intentions, individuals can reprogramme their subconscious mind to support emotional growth and wellbeing.

While both auto-suggestions and hetero-suggestions can be valuable tools for personal growth and development, auto-suggestions may be more important for emotional awakening. By tapping into their own inner wisdom and intuition, individuals can cultivate a deeper understanding of themselves and their emotions, leading to greater self-awareness, self-confidence, and inner peace.

Beyond the Art of Oratory

When someone lacks effective communication skills, it can lead to misunderstandings, misinterpretations, and conflicts. Poor communication can strain relationships with friends, family, colleagues, and superiors. It can lead to feelings of frustration, resentment, and isolation, as messages may not be conveyed clearly or received as intended. In professional settings, ineffective communication can hinder teamwork and collaboration. Effective communication is vital for networking and career growth, and the lack of it may lead to missed opportunities. Individuals with poor communication skills may feel anxious or hesitant when expressing themselves, leading to low self-confidence.

Effective communication is not solely dependent on being an expert speaker. One of the most crucial elements of effective communication is active listening. It involves fully concentrating, understanding, responding, and remembering what others say. Moreover, non-verbal cues play a significant role in communication as well. Body language, facial expressions, eye contact, and gestures can convey emotions and intentions, sometimes more effectively than words alone. Understanding and acknowledging the emotions of others is vital for effective communication. Using simple language and avoiding jargon or complicated terms ensures that the message is easily understood by the audience. Adapting one's communication style to different situations and audiences is a mark of effective communication. Strong writing skills are equally important, especially in emails, reports, and other written forms of communication. By honing these abilities, individuals can become more successful in conveying their messages, connecting with others, and fostering positive relationships in various aspects of life.

Imagination and Creativity: Unleashing the Power of Innovative Thinking

Imagination is the natural and unguided ability to create mental images, ideas, or concepts. It often occurs without conscious effort and can be random, free-flowing, and unrestricted. Imagination can involve daydreaming, creative brainstorming, or envisioning scenarios without specific limitations.

Wavering of the mind, on the other hand, refers to a state of indecision or instability in one's thoughts or emotions. It involves being uncertain or hesitant or fluctuating in one's beliefs, decisions, or focus.

Controlled imagination is a vital cognitive tool that enables us to innovate, solve problems, and plan strategically. This involves intentionally guiding and directing one's creative thoughts and mental imagery. It is a more deliberate and focused process whereby you harness your imaginative abilities for a specific purpose or goal. Controlled imagination is often used in problem-solving, visualisation exercises, and creative endeavours with a defined objective in mind.

Creativity is a broader and more intrinsic quality related to the generation of novel and valuable ideas, solutions, or expressions. It is the ability to think outside the box, come up with original concepts, and make connections between seemingly unrelated elements. Creativity is a crucial quality for human beings, as it enables us to adapt and thrive in an ever-changing world. It is not limited to the arts but is relevant to all aspects of life, from scientific research to business innovation.

One of the main benefits of creativity is that it allows individuals to approach problems from different angles, leading to more diverse and effective solutions. It fosters curiosity, exploration, and experimentation, encouraging individuals to take risks and try new things. Moreover, creative thinking helps individuals develop a growth mindset, essential for personal growth and self-improvement.

Another crucial aspect of creativity is its ability to enhance communication and collaboration. Creative individuals can express themselves more clearly and effectively, facilitating better communication with others. Additionally, creative problem-solving requires input and collaboration from multiple perspectives, fostering teamwork and collective problem-solving.

Steve Jobs said, 'Creativity is just connecting things.' Linking observations from diverse books, watching thought-provoking films, visiting new places, and having meaningful conversations with different people can indeed yield creative results. This cross-pollination of ideas can lead to novel combinations and unique insights beyond the boundaries of individual sources.

Regular mindfulness practice can improve self-awareness, concentration, and the ability to observe thoughts, enhancing the imaginative process. Engaging in mental flexibility and visualising exercises also strengthens the creative faculties.

Imagination is like a muscle that needs regular exercise. Dedicate time every day or week to creative activities, such as writing, drawing, storytelling, or problem-solving. Keeping a journal or sketchbook in which you jot down imaginative thoughts and ideas can also be helpful. This imaginative capacity can also act as a stress relief mechanism and enhance our empathy by allowing us to see the world from different perspectives.

By nurturing imagination and allowing it to interact with the creative process, one can unlock new avenues of innovation and expression.

Embrace Your Passion: Igniting the Flames of Success

Passion is the magical force that ignites the flames of inspiration and propels individuals towards a life of immense success and fulfilment. It is the inner fire that drives you to pursue your dreams with unwavering dedication and enthusiasm, transforming mere existence into a vibrant and purposeful journey. Embracing passion opens the doors to a truly successful life. Passion springs from the core of your being, reflecting your true purpose and calling in life. Embrace your uniqueness, talents, and interests, for within them lies the blueprint of your passion. Listen to the whispers of your heart and unleash the power of passion by dedicating yourself to what sets your soul on fire. Whether it's a creative pursuit, a meaningful cause, or a noble endeavour, immerse yourself wholeheartedly in your passion, for therein lies the path to extraordinary success.

In the pursuit of passion, obstacles may arise, but with unwavering grit, you can overcome them all. Passion fuels perseverance, enabling you to weather storms and rise stronger from challenges. Embrace setbacks as stepping stones on the road to success.

As you follow your dreams with conviction, you become a beacon of inspiration, encouraging others to pursue their passions and live authentically. A passion-fuelled life is marked by continuous learning and self-improvement, propelling you to new heights of success.

Passion knows no bounds; dare to dream big and envision a future beyond your wildest imagination. Allow your passion to fuel audacious goals, for it is within the realm of the extraordinary that you shall carve a path of remarkable success. A fabulous life of passion is rooted in gratitude and joy. Appreciate the beauty of each moment, cherish the journey, and savour the joy of pursuing what you love. Gratitude amplifies passion and adds sparkle to your path to success.

Passion is a force for positive change in the world. As you immerse yourself in your passion, let it become a vehicle for positive impact in the lives of others. Create a ripple effect of goodness and leave a lasting legacy of inspiration.

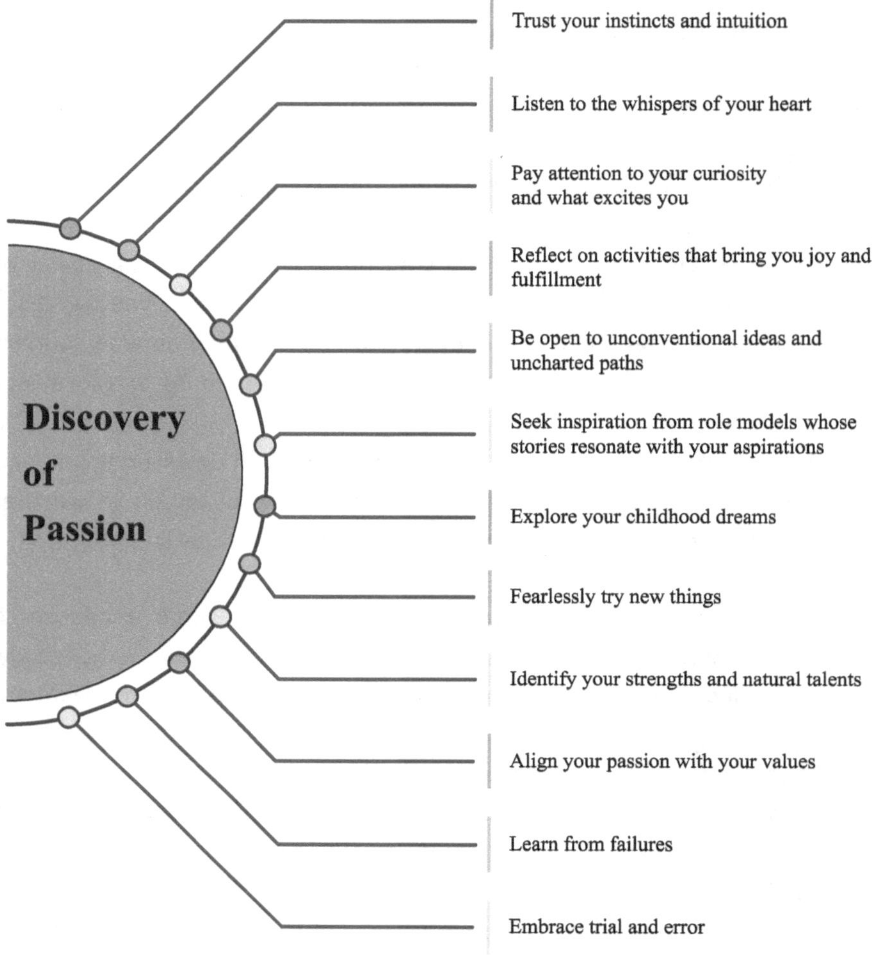

Conquering Procrastination

It can be tempting to put off tasks, especially those that are challenging or unpleasant, but the habit of procrastination can have negative consequences over time.

When we procrastinate, we may feel a temporary sense of relief or pleasure from avoiding the task at hand. However, this relief is often short-lived and can be followed by feelings of guilt, anxiety, and stress as the deadline for the task approaches. In addition to the negative emotional impact, procrastination can also lead to poor performance, missed opportunities, and decreased productivity.

Procrastination is like a slow poison because it can gradually erode our ability to achieve our goals and can lead to a sense of dissatisfaction with our lives. If we consistently put off important tasks, we may find that we are not making progress in our personal or professional lives, and we may miss out on opportunities to learn and grow.

To overcome the habit of procrastination, taking the first step is paramount. Begin by identifying the task or goal, breaking it down into smaller steps, and setting specific goals and deadlines. Create a detailed plan and eliminate distractions to maintain focus. Start with the easiest step to gain momentum and visualise success to boost motivation. Utilise time management techniques and reward yourself for each completed step. Stay accountable by sharing your goals with someone you trust, and practise self-compassion in times of setbacks. With persistence and consistent application of these strategies, you can conquer procrastination, achieve your goals, and experience a greater sense of efficiency and fulfilment in your endeavours. Remember, progress is a journey, and the first step sets the course for success. It is also important to identify the reasons you are procrastinating, like low self-esteem, having to perform under pressure, perfectionism, and non-prioritisation of tasks, and address any underlying issues, such as fear of failure or lack of motivation.

Desire and Greed

Desire can be a positive and motivating force that propels us to pursue our goals and aspirations. When we have healthy desires, they can provide us with a sense of purpose and fulfilment, leading to increased happiness and satisfaction. Desire can drive us to take action, overcome obstacles, and achieve personal growth, which contributes positively to our emotional well-being.

On the other hand, greed is an excessive and insatiable desire for more than what is necessary or reasonable. Greed is driven by an insatiable hunger for material possessions, wealth, or power, often at the expense of others. This excessive craving can lead to feelings of dissatisfaction, envy, and selfishness, negatively impacting emotional well-being. Greed can create a perpetual cycle of discontentment, compromising our ability to find true happiness and contentment.

In terms of overall well-being, it is important to distinguish between healthy desire and unhealthy greed. So, embracing healthy desires that align with our values and aspirations can positively impact our emotional well-being by providing motivation and fulfilment. However, succumbing to greed, which represents an insatiable and excessive desire for more, can lead to emotional turmoil, discontentment, and a diminished sense of well-being. Therefore, it is important to be mindful of our desires and intentions and to cultivate a sense of balance and moderation in our pursuit of them. Striking a balance between desire and contentment is essential for emotional well-being and a positive outlook.

Attitude Towards Change

'Change is the only constant in life.'
- Heraclitus

Change is an inherent part of life, and, whether we embrace it or not, it will inevitably occur. Individuals and industries that fail to adapt to new technologies and shifting trends risk falling behind and facing adverse consequences in the long run.

- In the mid-20th century, the New York Central Railroad was one of the most prominent railroads in the United States. However, the company resisted the shift to diesel-electric locomotives and continued to rely on steam-powered locomotives, which were less efficient and more expensive to operate. This unwillingness to modernise and adopt more advanced technologies led to financial troubles, and the New York Central Railroad eventually collapsed in 1968.

- Kodak once held a near-monopoly in the film and photography industry. In the 1970s, Kodak's own engineer, Steve Sasson, invented the digital camera, but the company was hesitant to invest in this technology due to concerns about its potential impact on their profitable film business. The company's failure to adapt to the changing market led to its decline and eventual bankruptcy.

- BlackBerry was once a dominant player in the smartphone market, known for its secure messaging and email capabilities. However, the company failed to innovate and adapt to the touchscreen smartphone revolution initiated by Android devices and Apple's iPhone. This led to a decline in popularity and market share, almost pushing BlackBerry to bankruptcy.

These incidents serve as reminders that being open to change and innovation is essential for progress and survival.

The unwillingness to change is a mental attitude or belief system that resists the idea of making changes to one's behaviour, habits, or beliefs. This mindset can be a significant obstacle to personal growth and development as well as to success in various areas of life.

Individuals with an unwillingness to change may hold onto beliefs or habits that are no longer serving them, even if they are aware that these behaviours are harmful or ineffective. They may feel threatened by the idea of change, perceiving it as a challenge to their identity or a sign of weakness. This can lead to a sense of stagnation, frustration, and even resentment towards those who advocate change.

There are several reasons why people may develop an unwillingness to change. For example, they may have had negative experiences in the past that have made them fearful of change, or they may be overly attached to their comfort zones and resistant to the idea of stepping outside of them. Additionally, they may lack the necessary skills or resources to implement change effectively, leading to feelings of helplessness or hopelessness.

Overcoming an unwillingness to change requires a willingness to challenge one's own beliefs and assumptions, as well as a commitment to personal growth and development. This may involve seeking out new information, practising new behaviours, and developing new skills. It may also require support from others, such as friends, family members, or a therapist.

Ultimately, changing one's mindset from one that is characterised by an unwillingness to change to one of openness and growth can be a powerful catalyst for personal transformation and a more fulfilling life. It may require effort and persistence, but the rewards can be significant, including increased confidence, resilience, and a sense of purpose.

Embracing a Balanced Competitive Spirit and Overcoming the False Mindset of Comparison

A competitive spirit can be beneficial when adopted critically and in a balanced manner. It serves to motivate individuals to strive for excellence and push their boundaries, fostering innovation, progress, and personal growth. Engaging in healthy competition exposes individuals to diverse perspectives, promoting learning and adaptability. Moreover, it builds resilience, grit, and a sense of accountability, encouraging goal-setting and effective time management. In a positive competitive environment, collaboration and teamwork thrive, leading to collective achievements.

When individuals constantly make comparisons and engage in competition, it can lead to the formation of a false mindset. Constantly comparing oneself to others may lead to feelings of inadequacy and inferiority, as self-worth becomes tied to external validation. A relentless focus on winning can instil a fear of failure, hindering personal growth and exploration of new opportunities. Dependence on external approval can develop, perpetuating the need for validation from others. Unhealthy competition can emerge, leading to rivalries and avoidance of collaboration. A scarcity mentality may take hold, fostering a zero-sum perspective that limits success. As a result, one may lose one's individuality and set unrealistic expectations for oneself and others.

Overcoming this comparison mindset that compels one to engage in unnecessary competition requires a meticulous approach. Start by cultivating self-awareness and recognising when you find that you are comparing yourself to or feeling the pressure to compete with others. Embrace your uniqueness and celebrate your individuality, understanding that everyone has their own strengths and weaknesses. Set realistic goals for personal growth and measure your progress against your past self rather than others. Limit your exposure to social media, as it often fosters unrealistic comparisons. Practise gratitude to shift your focus away from comparison and appreciate what you have achieved. Surround yourself with supportive and encouraging individuals who inspire you without promoting unhealthy competition. Instead of competing, view others as sources of inspiration and learning and try to gain insights from their journeys. Focus on collaborating and building strong relationships rather than trying to outdo others. Practise self-compassion, treating yourself kindly during setbacks and challenges. Adopt a growth mindset, seeing challenges as opportunities for learning and improvement. By being meticulous in applying these steps, you can gradually overcome the false mindset and embrace a more fulfilling and positive approach to life.

Over-attachment and Independence: Strike a Balance

Attachment is a fundamental aspect of human nature that plays a critical role in our lives. It forms the basis of emotional bonding, creating a sense of security and comfort in close relationships. Attachment fosters a sense of belonging and connectedness, strengthening our social support network and contributing to our identity. It fuels caring and compassionate behaviour, motivating us to support and care for others. Healthy attachment can also inspire personal growth and improvement, as we strive to maintain and enhance our relationships.

Overcoming over-attachment and over-expectation is essential for our emotional well-being and personal growth and for healthy relationships. When we are overly attached to certain outcomes or individuals, we become emotionally dependent, making us vulnerable to distress and disappointment when things don't go as planned. Likewise, having unrealistic expectations puts unnecessary pressure on us and on others, setting the stage for disappointment and dissatisfaction.

For emotional well-being, letting go of over-attachment allows us to develop emotional resilience and inner peace. When we can detach from specific outcomes, we become more adaptable and better equipped to cope with life's ups and downs. It fosters a sense of contentment and self-acceptance, reducing stress and anxiety.

Releasing ourselves from over-attachment and unrealistic expectations opens up space for exploration and learning. We become more open to new experiences and ideas, thus fostering self-development and self-discovery. This enables us to embrace change and seize opportunities for growth and improvement.

In relationships, overcoming over-attachment fosters healthier connections. It allows us to appreciate people for who they are without placing unrealistic demands on them. When we let go of rigid expectations, we allow room for genuine understanding, empathy, and compassion, strengthening our bonds with others.

Striking the right balance between attachment and independence allows us to enjoy the benefits of meaningful connections while retaining our individuality and emotional autonomy.

Happiness and Peace: States of Mind

Happiness is not just a fleeting emotion or constant euphoria: it is a state of mind characterised by contentment, well-being, and a positive outlook on life. It is a complex interplay of biological, psychological, and environmental factors. While external circumstances can influence momentary happiness, lasting happiness often originates from within.

Happiness is influenced by a combination of intrinsic and extrinsic factors. Intrinsic factors include personal values, self-acceptance, and a sense of purpose. Extrinsic factors include external events, social relationships, and material possessions. Balancing these factors and understanding their relative importance can impact one's overall state of happiness.

The pursuit of happiness is an ongoing journey rather than a destination. It involves setting meaningful goals, finding fulfilment in the process, and maintaining a positive attitude despite challenges. This pursuit can be enhanced by fostering a growth mindset and focusing on experiences rather than material possessions.

Peace is not merely the absence of conflict or chaos; it is an inner state of tranquillity, harmony, and equanimity. It is a sense of inner balance and serenity, even amid external disturbances. Peace arises from understanding and accepting the impermanence and unpredictability of life. One key aspect of attaining peace is learning to let go of attachments and expectations. Often, clinging to desires and the fear of loss can create inner turmoil. Embracing impermanence and practising non-attachment can lead to a more profound sense of peace.

Mindfulness, the practice of being fully present in the moment without judgment, is a powerful tool in achieving both happiness and peace. Mindfulness helps individuals connect with their inner selves, be aware of their emotions, and respond consciously to life's challenges.

Achieving happiness and peace requires a balance between nurturing the inner world of thoughts and emotions and engaging harmoniously with the outer world of relationships and experiences. Striking this equilibrium allows individuals to find joy and contentment amidst life's ups and downs.

Finding meaning and purpose in life is a fundamental aspect of experiencing happiness and peace. Engaging in activities that align with one's values and contribute to the well-being of others fosters a deeper sense of fulfilment and inner calm.

Recognising that life is imperfect and embracing both successes and failures with acceptance can foster resilience and inner peace. Imperfections are an inherent part of the human experience and acknowledging them can lead to self-compassion and emotional well-being.

Happiness and peace are indeed states of mind, intricately woven with the fabric of our thoughts, perceptions, and attitudes. While external circumstances may influence these states, cultivating an inner understanding, gratitude, and mindful awareness plays a vital role in allowing us to experience lasting happiness and peace.

Self-confidence and Resilience: A Real Asset for Well-being and Happiness

Self-confidence and resilience are two important qualities that are closely related and can greatly impact an individual's life.

Self-confidence is the belief in one's abilities and qualities. It is a sense of assurance and trust in oneself that allows individuals to take risks and pursue their goals. When individuals are self-confident, they tend to have a positive outlook on life and are more likely to succeed in their personal and professional endeavours.

Resilience, on the other hand, refers to an individual's ability to bounce back from setbacks and difficult situations. It is the capacity to recover from adversity, adapt to change, and move forward in the face of challenges. Resilient individuals are able to maintain a positive attitude and persevere through obstacles, and this can greatly contribute to their success in life.

The relationship between self-confidence and resilience is such that self-confidence can help to build resilience and resilience can enhance self-confidence. When individuals are self-confident, they are more likely to approach challenges with a positive attitude and persevere through difficulties, which can help to build resilience. At the same time, when individuals are resilient, they are better able to cope with setbacks and failures, which can help boost their self-confidence.

Self-confidence and resilience can be achieved through various strategies, including setting achievable goals, practising self-compassion, seeking support from others, learning from failures and mistakes, and cultivating a growth mindset. By developing these qualities, individuals can increase their chances of success and well-being, even in the face of challenges and adversity.

In summary, self-confidence and resilience are two important qualities that can greatly impact an individual's life. By building self-confidence and resilience, individuals can increase their ability to overcome challenges, pursue their goals, and lead a fulfilling life.

Satisfaction

Satisfaction is indeed a real asset, as it can greatly impact an individual's overall well-being and happiness. When individuals are satisfied with their lives, they tend to experience increased motivation, better relationships, and improved physical and mental health. Moreover, satisfaction can help individuals focus on what they have rather than what they lack, which can improve their overall sense of gratitude and happiness. When individuals are satisfied with their lives, they are less likely to engage in negative self-talk and rumination that can lead to stress, anxiety, and depression.

On the other hand, when individuals are not satisfied with their lives, they may experience a sense of emptiness, frustration, and despair. This can lead to feelings of hopelessness and can impact their mental and physical health negatively.

To cultivate a sense of satisfaction in life, individuals can focus on pursuing personal passions, prioritising self-care, and building supportive relationships. It is also important to develop a mindset of gratitude and to focus on the positive aspects of life, even in the face of challenges and difficulties.

Overcoming the Fear of Failure

Fear of failure can have a significant impact on an individual's life, profoundly affecting their personal and professional growth, relationships, and overall well-being. This insidious fear can manifest in various ways, leading to detrimental behaviours like procrastination, lack of self-confidence, negative self-talk, self-criticism, and avoidance. Its pervasive influence can hinder individuals from reaching their full potential and embracing life's opportunities with confidence.

To conquer the paralysing grip of the fear of failure, one must embrace a combination of self-awareness, resilience, and a willingness to learn and grow. By confronting this fear head-on, individuals can embark on a transformative journey towards greater success and fulfilment.

Strategies for Overcoming Fear of Failure:

- *Challenge negative self-talk*. Recognise and challenge the negative inner dialogue that feeds the fear of failure. Replace self-doubt with positive affirmations and constructive self-talk, empowering yourself to face challenges with optimism and determination.
- *Break down goals into achievable steps*. Transform daunting objectives into manageable tasks by breaking them down into smaller, more achievable steps. Celebrate each milestone accomplished, reinforcing your self-belief and motivation.
- *Focus on learning and growth*. Shift your perspective from that of fearing failure to that of embracing it as an opportunity for growth and learning. Reframe mistakes as valuable lessons, paving the way for continuous improvement and resilience.
- *Practise self-compassion*. Cultivate self-compassion and treat yourself with the same kindness and understanding you would extend to a friend. Embrace imperfections and setbacks as part of the human experience, fostering self-acceptance and resilience.

By implementing these strategies, anyone can embark on a transformative journey, transcending the fear of failure and embracing a life of greater success and fulfilment. With heightened self-awareness, unwavering resilience, and a dedication to learning and growth, individuals can cast aside the shackles of fear, unlock their true potential, and embrace life's challenges with newfound confidence and determination. Through this journey, they can foster meaningful relationships, unlock untapped opportunities, and attain personal growth and fulfilment.

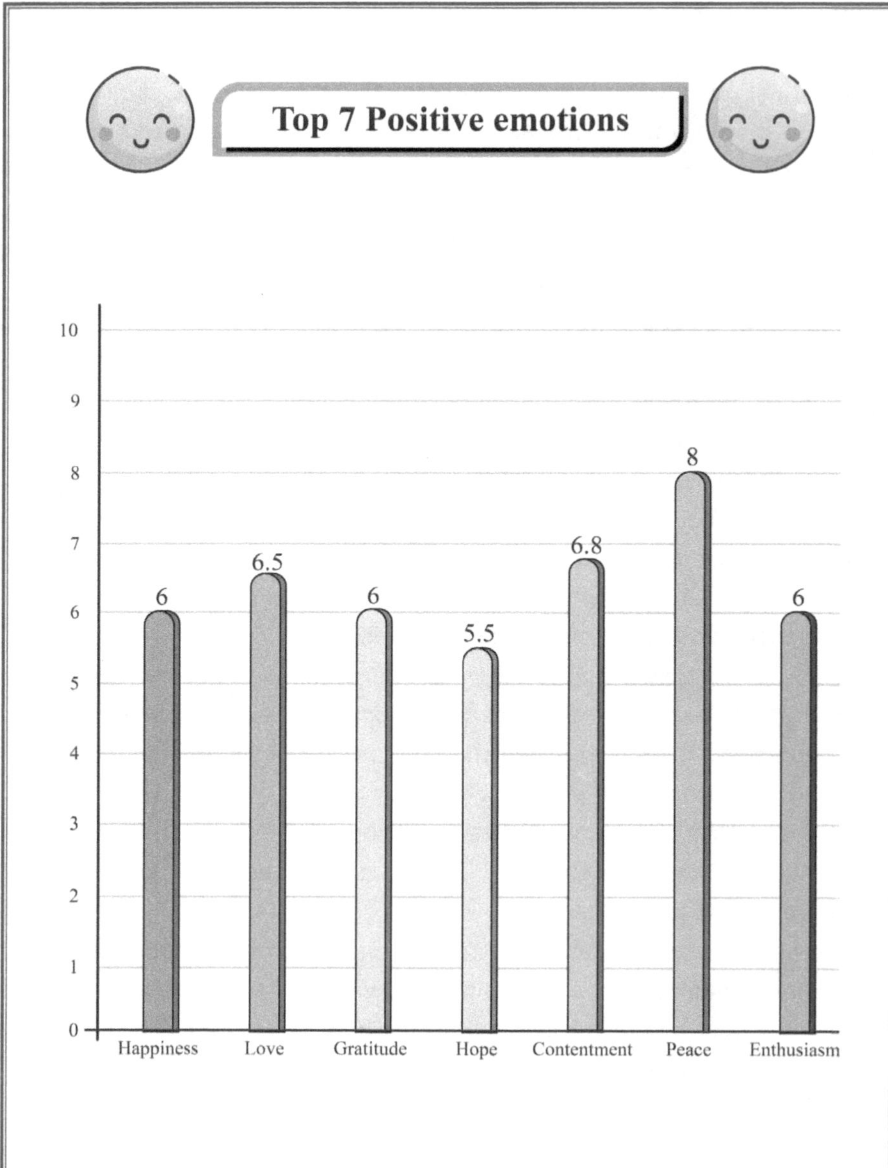

Top 7 Positive emotions
6
6.5
6
5.5
6.8
8
6
Happiness
Love
Gratitude
Hope
Contentment
Peace
Enthusiasm

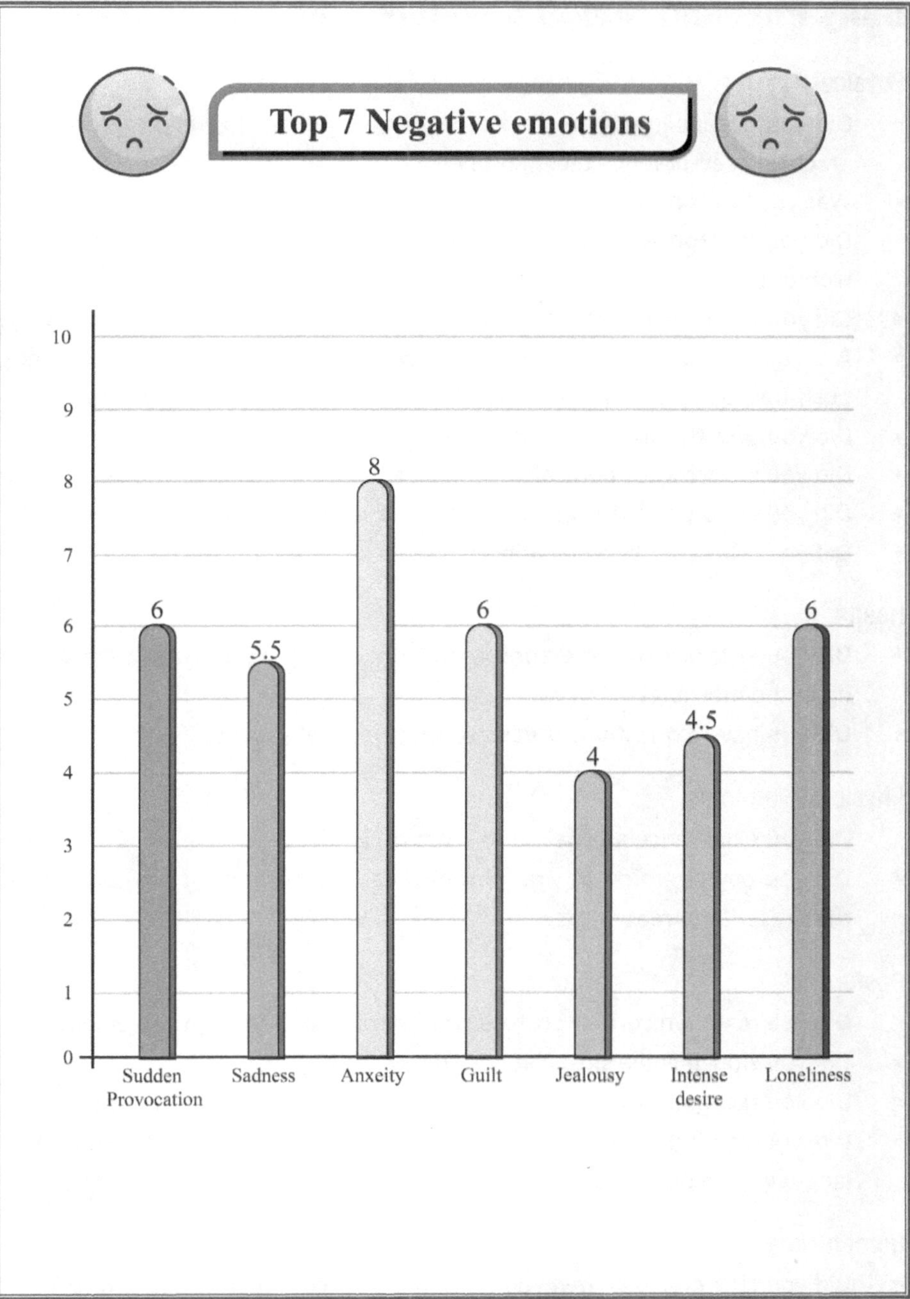

Top 7 Negative emotions
10
9
8
7
6
5
4
3
2
1
0
6
5.5
8
6
4
4.5
6
Sudden Provocation
Sadness
Anxeity
Guilt
Jealousy
Intense desire
Loneliness

Daily Physical Health Self-Assessment Checklist

Physical Activity

- Did you engage in regular physical activity—walking, jogging, exercising, or practising self-defence techniques?
- Was your walk mindful?
- Did you incorporate both aerobic and strength-training exercises into your workout?
- Did you warm up and cool down before and after your workout respectively?
- Are you familiar with short yet effective exercises such as planks, lunges, push-ups, quick yoga poses, suitable for those with time constraints?
- Did you take the stairs instead ofthe elevator(if possible)?
- Did you stretch your body after sitting for hours at a desk?
- Did you go to bed with light stomach after a leisurely walk?
- Did you relax your body by mind-scanning all your body parts?

Health

- Did you kickstart your metabolism by drinking a glass of water after waking up in the morning?
- Did you have a nutritious breakfast after physical activity?

Physical Symptoms

- Did you experience any pain or discomfort?
- Did you pay attention to your chronic health conditions (if any) and follow the prescribed treatments?

Posture

- Did you maintain correct posture while sitting, standing, and sleeping?
- Did you slouch while sitting at your desk/sofa?
- Did you recognise that your slouching is due to weakness or unawareness?
- Did you remind yourself that success is greatly influenced by your body language and posture?

Screen Time

- Did you take breaks to rest your eyes and reduce screen-related strain?
- Are you regularly rinsing your eyes with water?

Sun Exposure

- Did you enjoy being touched by the rays of the sun in the early morning/ evening?

Daily Emotional Health Self-Assessment Checklist

General

- Did you gauge the transformative potential of your morning rituals, including time blocking, preparing a to-do list, practising self-care, and continuous learning?
- Did you engage in nightly reflection to review both the positive aspects of your day and areas that require improvement or change?
- Did you ensure that your surroundings are conducive to your well-being/ goals?
- Did you embrace the idea of living in the present through your actions?
- Did you find and read productive materials?
- Did you identify your main sources of distraction?
- Were you aware that gadgets can be like double-edged swords, potentially causing harm if not used safely?
- Did you challenge anxious thoughts by asking yourself, 'What evidence do I have that this disastrous thing will happen?'

Mood

- Did you experience any significant changes in your mood throughout the day?
- Were you able to identify the reasons for these changes?

Stress Level

- Did you feel stressed or anxious today?
- Did you practise stress-reducing techniques, such as mindfulness or deep breathing?
- Did you limit excessive news consumption, which may lead to anxiety?
- Did you read a few pages of a good book before going to bed?

Relationships

- Did you experience any emotional challenges in your relationships with family, friends, or colleagues?

- Did you identify your energy drainers and keep away from them?
- Did you express your feelings and communicate effectively with others?

Emotional Support System

- Did you reach out for emotional support when needed, and did you offer support to others?
- Do you have a network of trusted individuals you can talk to about your feelings?

Self-Care

- Did you make time for self-care activities that bring you joy and relaxation?
- Did you engage in hobbies or activities that help you unwind?

Gratitude and Positive Moments

- Did you make note of positive experiences with gratitude throughout the day?

Emotional Triggers

- Were there any specific events or triggers that affected your emotional well-being?
- How did you respond to these triggers and could you find ways of managing them by using healthy coping mechanisms?

Self-Esteem

- How would you rate your self-esteem and self-worth today?
- Did you engage in positive self-talk and challenge negative thoughts?

Social Connections

- Did you interact with friends, family, or supportive individuals?
- Did you feel connected and nurtured by your social interactions?

Emotional Expression

- Were you able to express your emotions freely and appropriately?
- Did you suppress emotions that might need acknowledgment and expression?

Boundaries

- Did you set healthy boundaries with others to protect your emotional well-being?
- Did you respect the boundaries set by others?

Mindfulness and Relaxation
- Did you practise mindfulness or relaxation techniques to stay present and reduce anxiety?
- Did you engage in activities that help you unwind and de-stress?

Creative Expression
- Did you engage in creative activities that allow for emotional expression (e.g. writing, art, music)?

Emotional Goals/Others
- Did you identify areas where you want to improve emotionally?
- Did you perform your job enthusiastically/passionately?
- Did you document your knowledge/learning?

Checklist for Decision-Making on a Significant Scale
- Do you possess sufficient knowledge of and expertise in the subject?
- Will this decision have a direct impact on your health or the well-being of others?
- Are you making this decision out of laziness or a desire to take the easy route?
- Is the outcome of this decision minor or will it have profound, long-term implications in your life?
- Is your mind in a calm and focused state when making this decision?
- Are you making the decision out of greed, without considering the broader consequences?
- Have you had enough rest and sleep to ensure you're mentally and physically fit to decide?
- Have you chosen the right system or technique for addressing the issue?
- Are you adequately equipped, both in terms of resources and skills, to execute this decision?
- How will you manage your time to implement and follow through with this decision effectively?
- Are you aware of and addressing any cognitive distortions or biases that might influence your judgment?
- Should you seek expert opinions or advice before finalising this decision?

Checklist on Overcoming Fear

Addressing Past Trauma

- Are you aware that unwanted fear can have negative effects on thinking, decision-making, etc?
- Have you identified specific triggers from past experiences that contribute to your fear?
- Are you actively working on reframing and reshaping the memories you have that are associated with fear?

Facing Fearful Thoughts

- Have you identified your type of fear—is it a phobia, anticipatory anxiety, social anxiety, or something else?
- Have you examined the root causes of your fears and challenged their validity?
- Are you practising mindfulness meditation to realise and release fearful thoughts?
- Have you created a fear journal to track patterns and develop strategies with which to overcome them?

Building Determination

- Are you setting achievable milestones to gradually build determination?
- Have you established a daily routine that promotes mental stability and resilience?
- Are you exploring personal development resources to enhance your mindset and determination?

Participating in Activities

- Are you exploring a variety of activities to discover interests that resonate with you?
- Have you considered joining clubs or groups to share experiences and receive encouragement?
- Are you setting realistic expectations for yourself when participating in new activities?

Cultivating Positive Mindset

- Have you integrated gratitude practices into your daily routine to foster a positive mindset?
- Are you seeking inspiration from others who have successfully overcome similar fears?
- Have you developed a mantra or positive affirmation to reinforce a fearless outlook?

Affirmation and Empowerment

- Are you regularly engaging in activities that empower and boost your self-esteem?
- Have you acknowledged and celebrated progress, no matter how small, to reinforce positive change?
- Are you consciously choosing empowering language and thoughts to counteract feelings of helplessness?

Social Support

- Have you communicated your fears with friends or family members to strengthen your support network?
- Are you open to receiving constructive feedback and encouragement from those close to you?
- Have you considered joining online communities or forums where individuals share their experiences of overcoming similar fears?

Reflection and Adjustment

- Are you periodically reflecting on your fear journey to assess what strategies are effective?
- Have you adjusted your approach based on the evolving nature of your fears and progress?
- Are you actively seeking feedback from yourself and others to refine your fear-conquering strategies?

Checklist for Conquering Distractions

Effective Task Management

- Do you begin your day with a well-structured to-do list to guide your work and avoid aimless wandering?
- Have you organised tasks in a logical sequence to minimise confusion and reduce mental fatigue?
- Is your to-do list visually appealing and motivating, making you eager to tackle each item?
- Have you allocated specific time slots in your schedule for each task, preventing distractions from creeping in?

External Distractions

- Is your mobile silenced to eliminate unnecessary notifications that disrupt your focus?
- Have you informed colleagues that you prefer minimal interruptions during focused work periods?
- Do you set clear boundaries with friends, scheduling social interactions during breaks to prevent them from encroaching on your work time?

Prioritise and Conquer

- Have you prioritised tasks within your to-do list, identifying which ones require the most attention?
- Do you establish a clear order in which to tackle each task, ensuring you focus on the most important ones first?
- Are you committed to completing one task before moving on to the next, avoiding the temptation to multi task and lose focus?

Breaking Down the Big

- Do you break down complex tasks into smaller, more manageable parts to make them less daunting and more achievable?
- Have you developed a system to acknowledge and celebrate the completion of each task segment, boosting motivation for the remaining parts?

Taming the Mind

- Do you take regular moments to close your eyes and escape from external stimuli, allowing your mind to rest and recharge?

- Do you incorporate deep breathing exercises into your routine to calm your mind, release worries, and enhance focus?
- Have you made a habit of practising body relaxation techniques like resting/napping and stretching throughout the day to refresh your mind and maintain concentration?

Embrace the Present

- Are you constantly reminding yourself of the importance of the current task to maintain motivation and engagement?
- Have you cultivated a mindset that views each task as meaningful and deserving of your full attention, rather than a burden to be endured?
- Do you approach tasks with enthusiasm and dedication, treating them as opportunities for growth and accomplishment?
- Have you adopted a present-focused mindset, avoiding distractions by focusing on the task at hand rather than dwelling on the past or worrying about the future?

Vibrant Family

The family is an important building block of society. The family system is a vital social institution that has been present in societies across the world for centuries and provides emotional, social, and economic support to its members. One of the key functions of the family system is to provide comfort, encouragement, and empathy during difficult times. Family members celebrate each other's successes and achievements. The family system can also play a crucial role in fostering personal growth and development. Parents can teach children important values, skills, and social norms, and can help them develop a sense of identity and purpose. Similarly, adult family members can provide guidance and support as younger family members navigate important life transitions. It can also help provide financial stability to its members. By pooling resources and sharing expenses, family members can help each other in navigating economic hardships and achieve important financial goals. Families can play an important role in transmitting cultural traditions and values from one generation to the next. Through shared experiences, rituals, and traditions, families can help preserve and pass on important cultural knowledge and practices. The family system can provide a sense of belonging and connectedness that is crucial for human well-being. By fostering strong bonds between family members, the family system can help individuals feel supported and valued.

At the same time, when the family system deteriorates, it can have adverse impacts on society, culture, peace, and the economy. **When the family system deteriorates, it can contribute to a loss of cultural values and traditions, which can lead to a sense of cultural disconnection and a crisis of identity**, contributing to social problems such as poverty, crime, substance abuse, and mental health issues. This can negatively impact society as a whole, leading to increased healthcare costs, reduced productivity, and decreased social cohesion. It can contribute to conflict and violence both within the family and in the wider society. Family conflicts can spill over into the community and lead to higher levels of crime and violence. Children who grow up in unstable or abusive homes are more likely to engage in delinquent behaviours, including drug use and criminal activity.

The breakdown of the family system can have negative economic impacts. Children who grow up in unstable homes are more likely to struggle academically and may have difficulty finding employment later in life. This can lead to decreased productivity and lower economic growth overall. Mental health issues can also be linked to the breakdown of the family. Children who experience abuse, neglect, or instability in the home may be more likely to experience anxiety, depression, and other mental health problems. It is therefore important to prioritise efforts to support and strengthen families, which will lead to a stronger and more resilient society.

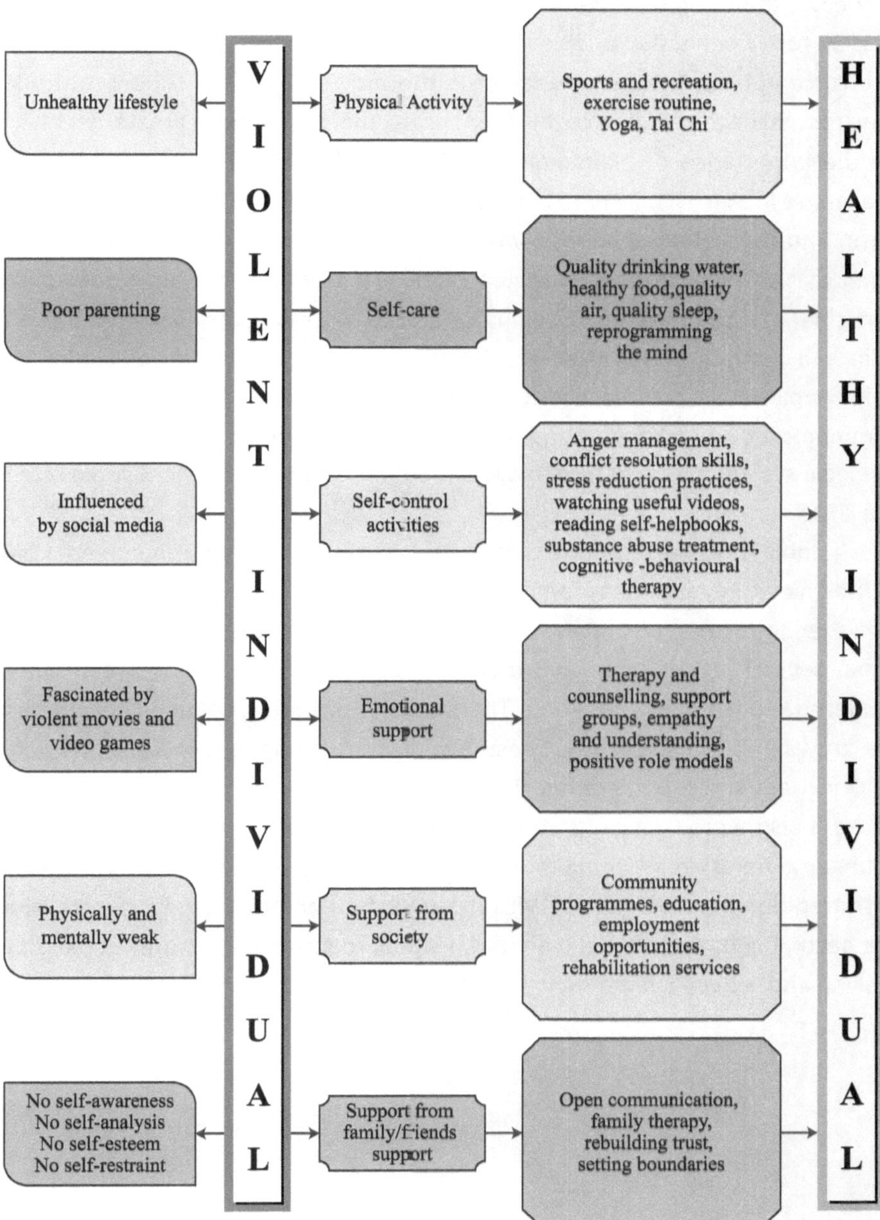
Unhealthy lifestyle
Poor parenting
Influenced by social media
Fascinated by violent movies and video games
Physically and mentally weak
No self-awareness
No self-analysis
No self-esteem
No self-restraint
VIOLENT INDIVIDUAL
Physical Activity
Self-care
Self-control activities
Emotional support
Support from society
Support from family/friends support
Sports and recreation, exercise routine, Yoga, Tai Chi
Quality drinking water, healthy food, quality air, quality sleep, reprogramming the mind
Anger management, conflict resolution skills, stress reduction practices, watching useful videos, reading self-helpbooks, substance abuse treatment, cognitive -behavioural therapy
Therapy and counselling, support groups, empathy and understanding, positive role models
Community programmes, education, employment opportunities, rehabilitation services
Open communication, family therapy, rebuilding trust, setting boundaries
HEALTHY INDIVIDUAL

In the US, the decline in the divorce rate from its peak of 5.3 per 1, 000 people in 1981 to 2.7 per 1, 000 people in 2020 implies that fewer marriages are ending in divorce in recent years. One factor in this may be a shift in cultural attitudes towards marriage and divorce. In recent years, there has been a greater emphasis on the importance of maintaining healthy relationships and working through challenges in marriage instead of simply ending the relationship when difficulties arise. Another potential factor contributing to the decline in the divorce rate in America is an increase in premarital counselling and education. Many couples now participate in premarital counselling or attend workshops to learn relationship skills and communication strategies before they get married. This education can help couples avoid some of the common pitfalls that can lead to divorce, such as communication breakdowns and financial disagreements. Of course, changes in the legal system may also have played a role in the decline in the divorce rate in the USA.

In India, it is worth noting that the family system remains an essential part of Indian culture, and many families still adhere to traditional values and norms. However, in recent years, there has been a shift in the way families function in India. Several factors have contributed to this change, including urbanisation, modernisation, and globalisation. The trends of individualism and consumerism are growing in Indian society. These trends are leading to a focus on personal achievement and success rather than communal values and social responsibility. There is also a growing generation gap between parents and children, with the younger generation adopting more westernised values and lifestyles that clash with traditional Indian values. With more women entering the workforce, they are becoming financially independent, leading to greater autonomy in decision-making and reduced dependence on the extended family.

Understanding Common Differences between Women and Men

There are some biological, psychological, and attitudinal differences that are commonly observed between men and women. While many men and women who do not fit neatly into traditional gender roles, by understanding the general trends we can better prepare our minds to communicate with and respond well to others and even ourselves and contribute to the establishment of an environment of acceptance, appreciation, and open-mindedness in which men and women can celebrate their differences and utilise them as strengths rather than sources of conflict. In doing so, they can collaborate in creating a harmonious and balanced partnership, grounded in mutual respect and love, thereby building stronger relationships, creating a more just and equitable society, and raising children who are happy, healthy, and well-adjusted. We need to create opportunities for both men and women to succeed, regardless of gender.

Biological Differences

Biological dissimilarities between men and women arise primarily from genetic and hormonal variations. At the genetic level, men typically possess one X and one Y chromosome (XY), while women have two X chromosomes (XX). This fundamental genetic distinction leads to differences in the development of secondary sexual characteristics, reproductive organs, and hormonal profiles.

Hormonally, men and women have differing levels of sex hormones. Testosterone, predominant in males, influences traits like muscle mass, body hair, and deepening of the voice. Oestrogen and progesterone are the primary female sex hormones, impacting features such as breast development, menstrual cycles, and fertility.

Psychological Differences

Cognitive and emotional disparities between men and women have been subjects of extensive research. While generalisations exist, it's important to note that individual variations are substantial. In terms of cognition, studies suggest that men may excel in spatial tasks, while women often exhibit strengths in verbal abilities and emotional intelligence. These differences may arise from a combination of societal, environmental, and biological factors.

Emotionally, women tend to be more expressive and attuned to social cues, which can make them more empathetic and responsive in interpersonal relationships. Men, on the other hand, might exhibit a greater inclination towards risk-taking behaviour, possibly linked to evolutionary pressures. Again, these traits are not absolute and vary widely among individuals.

Attitudinal Differences

Attitudinal distinctions between men and women encompass factors like priorities, communication styles, and problem-solving approaches. Traditionally, men have been associated with assertiveness, competitiveness, and a focus on career advancement. Women, on the other hand, may prioritise nurturing, relationships, and communal well-being. However, contemporary societal shifts have blurred these lines considerably, leading to more fluid and diverse expressions of attitudes across genders.

Communication styles can also vary, with men sometimes favouring directness and succinctness, while women might emphasise rapport-building and nuanced expression. Problem-solving strategies can differ as well, with men sometimes gravitating towards analytical, task-oriented approaches, while women may lean towards collaborative, holistic methods.

Understanding Married Life

Two Fundamental Principles

1. There are biological, psychological, and attitudinal differences between men and women.
2. There is no perfect partner in any married couple, as each individual is unique.

As there are biological, psychological, and attitudinal differences between men and women, it's important to recognise and appreciate these differences instead of trying to change your partner or mould them into your own ideal. By understanding and accepting your partner's unique traits, you can better communicate and work with them to overcome challenges in your relationship. A successful marriage requires mutual respect between partners. This means treating your partner with kindness, empathy, and understanding, and valuing their opinions and contributions. It's important to avoid belittling, criticising, or disrespecting your partner, as this can erode trust and cause resentment. It's important to establish open and honest communication lines with your partner and to actively listen to their thoughts, feelings, and concerns. This can help you build trust and intimacy in your relationship and can prevent misunderstandings and conflicts from escalating.

No one is perfect, and it's important to accept your partner's flaws and imperfections. This means letting go of unrealistic expectations and embracing your partner for who they are. By accepting your partner's strengths and weaknesses, you can build a deeper, more meaningful connection in your relationship. Hence, marriage requires compromises from both partners. This means finding common ground and working together to find solutions to problems or conflicts. It's important to be willing to make sacrifices for your partner while also respecting your own needs and boundaries.

If family members are aware of these fundamental principles, they work on changing themselves instead of trying to change others.

Choosing a Life Partner

The most important qualities for a happy and fulfilling life partnership are trustworthiness, communication, respect, empathy, shared values, flexibility, emotional intelligence, and a sense of humour. By embodying these qualities, partners can build a strong, loving, and supportive relationship that can withstand the tests of time.

Choosing a life partner is a significant decision that will impact one's life greatly, so it's essential to consider various factors, such as values and beliefs, communication styles, compatibility in terms of interests, personalities, and lifestyles, trust in and respect for each other, family backgrounds, and future plans. Having similar financial goals and financial habits also plays an important role. But trust your intuition when selecting a partner for marriage. If something feels off, take the time to evaluate your options and make the best decision for yourself. Bear in mind that, even after careful selection, there will be differences of opinion between the two of you. If you are physically and emotionally balanced, you will be able to manage those differences successfully.

There are numerous factors that can contribute to the ruin of relationships, such as lack of communication, which starts with misunderstandings, unresolved conflicts, and feelings of resentment, infidelity, financial stress and disagreements over money, lack of intimacy and a connection, incompatibility, unrealistic expectations, lack of commitment and effort, substance abuse and addiction, domestic violence and abuse, differing values and goals, etc.

When both partners are emotionally and physically healthy, they are better able to cope with the challenges of life and to support each other through difficult times. This can help prevent conflict and resentment and can make the relationship more resilient.

Emotionally and physically healthy individuals are often more resilient in facing the challenges that arise in a marriage. Even the healthiest individuals and couples may face unforeseen circumstances or external factors that strain their relationship. However, when both partners are emotionally and physically healthy, they are better equipped to face these challenges together, seek support when needed, and work towards resolving issues rather than resorting to divorce as a solution.

Loneliness

Loneliness is strongly associated with depression, anxiety, and other mental health problems. Studies have shown that lonely people are more likely to experience symptoms of these disorders than those who are socially connected. Long-term loneliness is also linked to cognitive decline, including memory loss, difficulty concentrating, and decreased problem-solving abilities. Loneliness is associated with a range of physical health problems, including high blood pressure, heart disease, weakening of the immune system, and obesity. Lonely people may turn to alcohol or drugs to cope with their feelings of isolation and disconnection, which can lead to substance abuse and addiction. Loneliness can also disrupt sleep patterns, making it harder for people to fall asleep or stay asleep through the night. Research has shown that loneliness can actually reduce lifespan, with some studies finding that it can be as harmful as smoking or obesity.

Issues Faced by Unmarried Partners

According to data from the U. S. Census Bureau, the percentage of households headed by unmarried partners increased from 0.9% in 1960 to 8% in 2020.

The culture of non-marital partnerships can create a range of challenges and limitations that may affect individuals in different ways, depending on their circumstances, culture, and personal beliefs. Unmarried partners do not have the same legal protections as married couples. This means that if one partner becomes ill or dies, the other partner may not have any legal right to make medical decisions for them or inherit assets. This can create legal and financial issues in the event of a break-up, separation, or death. Unmarried partners may face challenges in terms of financial stability, particularly if they are not both contributing equally to household expenses or savings. Without legal protections or financial agreements, one partner may be more vulnerable to economic hardship, debt, or financial abuse. In some cultures or communities, non-marital partnerships may be stigmatised or frowned upon, leading to social isolation, discrimination, or even harassment. Unmarried partners may not have access to certain benefits or privileges that are reserved for married couples, such as health insurance, tax benefits, or parental rights. This can create practical difficulties and limit one's options and opportunities.

The Journey of Married Life

Married life is a journey that consists of different phases—the honeymoon phase, the adjustment phase, the parenting phase, the growth phase, the mid life phase, the retirement phase, and the senior phase. Each phase has different characteristics. During the honeymoon phase, couples are typically in a state of excitement and euphoria, enjoying each other's company and discovering new things about each other. However, after this period comes a time of adjustment and transition as they learn to navigate the ups and downs of married life. It's important to have realistic expectations about your marriage and your partner. Recognise that no relationship is perfect and that there will be challenges and disagreements along the way. Make time to do things together that you both enjoy. This can help strengthen your bond and deepen your connection with each other. No one is perfect, and it's important to be able to forgive your partner when they make mistakes or hurt your feelings. Remember that forgiveness is not the same as forgetting, but rather a way of letting go of anger and resentment and moving forward. Take time to appreciate your partner and the things that you love about your relationship. Take all possible steps to resolve the differences within yourself. As stated previously, if you maintain physical and emotional stability, nothing is impossible.

Happiness in a Marriage

Happiness is indeed a crucial aspect of a fulfilling married life. When both partners in a marriage are happy, it creates a strong foundation for a harmonious and lasting relationship. Happiness in marriage is a continuous journey that requires effort, understanding, and commitment from both partners. It is about nurturing the relationship, prioritising each other's happiness, and working together to create a loving and joyful life together.

However, it is important to note that achieving happiness in marriage is a complex and multifaceted endeavour, and it can vary from couple to couple based on their unique dynamics, values, and expectations.

Happiness in marriage is closely linked to improved physical health. Studies have shown that happily married individuals tend to have lower levels of stress, better-functioning immune systems, and reduced risk of chronic illnesses. The emotional support and companionship provided by a happy marriage contribute positively to overall well-being.

A happy marriage provides a solid foundation on which the storms of life can be weathered together. Difficulties and conflicts are inevitable in any relationship, but when a couple is genuinely happy, they are better equipped to handle challenges as a united front. Happiness strengthens resilience and helps couples navigate obstacles with patience, understanding, and problem-solving skills.

But there are many ways in which partners can spoil their shared happiness, even for trivial reasons. Poor communication can lead to misunderstandings, misinterpretations, and a lack of understanding between partners. Even during happy occasions, failing to effectively communicate needs, expectations, or emotions can result in conflicts. Lingering unresolved conflicts or resentments can taint the atmosphere during otherwise joyous occasions. If past issues have not been properly addressed and resolved, they may resurface. Certain actions, words, or situations can trigger negative emotions in individuals, leading to spontaneous reactions that can ruin the moment. These triggers can be rooted in past experiences, insecurities, or personal sensitivities. People who have negative thinking patterns tend to focus on the bad things in life and expect the worst. This can lead them to see even happy occasions in a negative light and search for things to complain about. People with low self-esteem often feel like they don't deserve to be happy. This can lead them to sabotage their own happiness, either consciously or unconsciously. Change can be scary, and some people may try to avoid it by spoiling happy occasions because they are afraid of what might happen if things change for the better. Unrealistic expectations of how a happy occasion should unfold can lead to disappointment. If one partner's expectations are not met, they may react negatively and spoil the happiness for themselves and others.

Partners may bring their own personal issues and external stressors into the relationship. These can include work-related stress, financial difficulties, health problems, or other life challenges. If these issues are not effectively managed, they can affect the overall happiness and harmony within the relationship. Open and honest communication is key to resolving any problems in a relationship. It is also important to be patient and understanding, as change takes time. If you are both willing to work on the relationship, you can overcome any obstacle and create a happy and fulfilling marriage.

It's important to remember that happiness in marriage is not a constant state, and challenges may arise along the way. Ultimately, fostering happiness in a marriage is an ongoing journey that requires dedication, patience, and the willingness to nurture the relationship.

Conflict Communication Skills

Effective conflict communication skills are crucial for a happy married life because they allow couples to resolve their differences in a healthy and productive way. When couples are able to communicate effectively during conflict, they are better able to understand each other's perspectives, find common ground, and compromise. When your spouse expresses concerns or disagrees with you, actively listen to their perspective. Listen without interrupting and pay attention to what your partner is saying, both verbally and nonverbally. For example, if your spouse says, 'I'm not happy with the division of household chores, ' you can respond by saying, 'I hear that you're not happy with the current arrangement. Can you tell me more about what you'd like to see changed?'

When expressing your own concerns or feelings, use 'I' statements instead of 'you' statements. This can help prevent the conversation from becoming accusatory or defensive. For example, instead of saying, 'You never help with the housework, ' you could say, 'I feel overwhelmed with the amount of housework and would appreciate more help.'

Conflict resolution involves finding a solution that works for both parties. This requires compromise and a willingness to negotiate. For example, if you and your spouse disagree on how to spend money, you could suggest a compromise of setting a budget and finding ways to cut expenses that you both agree on.

When you are arguing, it is important to focus on the issue at hand, not on your partner's personality or character. This will help you stay calm and avoid getting personal.

When you make a mistake or say something hurtful during a disagreement, it's important to apologise sincerely. This can help repair the relationship and prevent further conflicts. For example, if you said something hurtful during an argument, you could say, 'I'm sorry for what I said earlier. I didn't mean to hurt you.'

Decision-making as a Couple

Often, we may find situations arising that lead to a conflict between our rational, logical brain (often associated with the prefrontal cortex) and our emotional, impulsive brain (often associated with the amygdala and other parts of the limbic system). When faced with the need to make a decision, our rational brain may weigh the pros and cons of each option and make a logical choice, i.e. good/bad, while our emotional brain may prioritise our gut instincts or immediate desires, i.e. like/dislike. This can lead to an internal conflict wherein our rational brain and emotional brain are vying for control over the decision-making process, which can cause procrastination or indecision.

In reality, our brains work in a complex and integrated way to help us make decisions based on a variety of factors, including our past experiences, values, and goals. To resolve the conflict between the rational and the emotional brain, one has to become more aware of one's own thoughts and emotions. When we are aware of what is going on inside us, it is easier to make decisions that are in line with our values and goals. Another thing that we can do is slow down and take our time when making decisions. Rushing into a decision can lead to choices that we later regret. By taking our time, we gives ourselves the opportunity to weigh all of our options and make the best possible decision.

Ultimately, the balance between our rational and emotional brains will vary depending on the situation and our level of self-awareness.

Making decisions as a couple is not always easy, but it is an important part of building a strong relationship. **When two partners have to make a decision, there are four brains involved in the process, i.e. the two rational brains and the two emotional brains.** In these situations, it is important for the partners to communicate openly and honestly with each other. They need to listen to each other's perspectives and try to understand where the other person is coming from. They also need to be willing to compromise. In some cases, the partners may need to put their own personal preferences aside and make a decision that is in the best interests of the family as a whole. If you and your partner disagree on a decision, don't take it personally. Remember that you are on the same team and that you are both trying to make the best decision for the family. It takes time to learn how to make decisions together. Be patient with each other and with the process.

Managing Relationships with In-laws

It can be challenging to maintain healthy relationships with your in-laws, but it is an important part of a happy married life. It's important to set boundaries with your in-laws. This can include setting limits on the amount of time you spend with them, the topics of conversation, and what is considered acceptable behaviour. Instead of dwelling on the negative aspects of your relationship with your in-laws, focus on the positives. Look for common interests or shared experiences that can help strengthen your bond. Showing appreciation and gratitude can go a long way in building positive relationships with in-laws. This can include expressing gratitude for their help or support and acknowledging their positive qualities. Respect is essential in any relationship, and this includes relationships with in-laws. Treat them with respect and kindness, even if you don't always see eye-to-eye. It's important to remember that everyone has their own quirks and personality traits, including in-laws. Don't take their behaviour or comments personally, and try to approach situations with a level head. Be open and honest with your in-laws, but also be respectful of and patient with their feelings and opinions, exhibiting a willingness to understand their point of view and work on the relationship.

When Both Partners Go to Work

Managing work and family responsibilities can be challenging when both partners are working, but with some careful planning and communication, it's possible to lead a successful and happy life. It's important to identify what's most important to you and your family and prioritise those things. This might mean sacrificing certain activities or events to make time for work or family obligations. Creating a schedule or routine can help you manage your time more effectively. This might include setting specific times for work, family activities, and household chores. It is essential that both partners share responsibilities for household tasks and child care. This can help prevent one partner from feeling overwhelmed or resentful and can also help build a sense of teamwork and collaboration. Being flexible is important when managing work and family responsibilities. Unexpected events can arise, and it's important to be willing to adjust your plans as needed. Be open and honest with your partner about your needs and expectations and be willing to compromise and make adjustments as needed. Don't be afraid to seek support from family and friends. Most importantly, taking care of yourself is essential when managing work and family responsibilities. Make time for activities that you enjoy and prioritise self-care activities like exercise and relaxation. Remember, when you are attentive to the five inner care elements, i.e. food, water, air, sleep, and thoughts, and possess a strong body and strong mind, anything is possible.

Impact of Habits that Prioritise Temporary Pleasure

There are many temporary pleasures that can ruin our physical and emotional health in married life if we make the pursuit of them a habit. These include:

- *Addiction.* Addiction to drugs, alcohol, or gambling can have a devastating impact on a marriage, leading to financial problems, infidelity, and violence. Social media addiction, meanwhile, can lead to isolation from one's spouse and family. It can also lead to comparisons with others, which can cause low self-esteem and depression.
- *Overspending.* Overspending can lead to debt, financial stress, and arguments about money.

There are many more such habits, and their effects include:

- *Diminished intimacy.* Seeking temporary pleasures outside the marriage, whether through infidelity or excessive indulgence of personal hobbies or interests, can lead to a decline in intimacy and emotional connection. This can result in feelings of loneliness, dissatisfaction, and a lack of fulfilment within the relationship.
- *Erosion of trust.* Indulging in temporary pleasures often involves secrecy and deception, which erode trust within a marriage. Trust is a vital foundation

for a healthy relationship, and when it is broken, feelings of betrayal, resentment, and emotional distress arise.

- *Communication breakdowns*. Pursuing temporary pleasures may result in a breakdown of effective communication between partners. Instead of addressing underlying issues or engaging in open dialogue, individuals may choose to avoid difficult conversations or resort to passive-aggressive behaviour. This lack of healthy communication can cause emotional distance and hinder the resolution of conflicts.
- *Neglecting responsibilities*. Indulging in temporary pleasures often involves prioritising immediate gratification over long-term well-being.

The identification of triggers is an important step to overcoming such habits. What are the things that trigger your unhealthy habits? Once you know your triggers, you can start to make a plan for how you are going to overcome your unhealthy habits. This plan should include specific steps that you will take to avoid your triggers and build healthier habits. Instead of indulging the habit, find some healthy substitutes that will give you pleasure. This could be something like exercising, spending time with loved ones, or pursuing a hobby.

To maintain a healthy married life, it is essential to prioritise long-term well-being over immediate gratification. This involves cultivating healthy habits, open communication, trust-building, and addressing any underlying issues that may contribute to the pursuit of temporary pleasures.

Food and Family

Home-cooked food can play a vital role in creating and maintaining strong family bonds. Cooking and eating together can be shared experiences that bring family members closer, providing opportunities for families to communicate. Home-cooked meals often involve traditional family recipes that have been passed down from generation to generation. Sharing these recipes and cooking together can help keep these traditions alive and provide a sense of connection to family history.

Eating together can create a sense of love and closeness and help family members stay connected with one another. The hormones associated with love are oxytocin and vasopressin. These hormones promote social bonding, trust, and attachment. Love also can help reduce stress, improve mood, and promote overall well-being.

Home-cooked meals can be healthier than eating out or relying on processed foods. When families cook and eat together, they can prioritise nutrition and make sure everyone is getting the nutrients they need to be healthy and happy.

Cooking and eating meals together should be enjoyable. So relax, have fun, and make some memories that will last a lifetime.

Packed Meals

Freshly cooked meals are often more nutritious than packed meals because they contain more essential nutrients like vitamins, minerals, and antioxidants. These nutrients can degrade over time, and packaged meals may not be able to retain them for long periods. Packed meals may contain preservatives, additives, and other chemicals that may not be healthy in the long term. Artificial ingredients have been linked to various health problems like allergies, hyperactivity, and even cancer. Moreover, packed meals may not be safe to eat if they are not stored at the correct temperature. Eating spoiled or contaminated food can lead to foodborne illnesses, which can cause symptoms like diarrhoea, vomiting, and fever.

In general, outside food is likely to be less nutritious and higher in calories, salt, sugar, and unhealthy fats. Overconsumption of unhealthy food can lead to health problems like obesity, diabetes, heart disease, and other chronic illnesses. Eating out regularly can also be expensive and may not be sustainable for all families. It may even lead to a sense of disconnection from one's cultural roots and traditions.

Rooftop Farming

Food contamination and adulteration are multifaceted concerns that can manifest at any stage from farm to table. Commencing at the farm, pesticides and fertilisers, if not judiciously administered, may leave residues on produce. Additionally, unscrupulous practices may lead to the adulteration of food products with substandard or harmful substances. During processing and handling, poor sanitation and cross-contamination can introduce deleterious substances or serve as opportunities for adulteration. Inadequate temperature control during transportation might lead to spoilage, bacterial proliferation, or further adulteration. In distribution and retail, mishandling or mislabelling can pose risks, while intentional adulteration further compounds the issue of food safety. At home, consumer handling is pivotal; failure to practise safe food preparation and storage can result in contamination or unwittingly consuming adulterated products. Natural contaminants, such as toxins or allergens, also warrant attention.

Rooftop farming can be a great way to add beauty, freshness, and a sense of community to a home. It can provide families with access to fresh home grown fruits and vegetables. Cultivating plants on one's roof can help improve air quality by filtering out pollutants and providing oxygen. A rooftop garden can provide a peaceful and relaxing space where families can escape the hustle and bustle of everyday life and get some exercise. Spending time in nature has also been shown to improve mental health. Plants must be chosen based on their suitability to your climate and growing conditions, factoring in the availability of sunlight and water, and light weight materials must be chosen to safeguard the stability of the roof. There are many experienced professionals who can help you design, install, and maintain a successful rooftop garden.

Two major benefits of rooftop cultivation are that the fruits and vegetables thus cultivated are:

1.   Free from chemicals and pesticides.
2.   More nutritious and fresh.

Taking Care of Aging Parents

Taking care of aging parents is a way of showing gratitude for all the sacrifices and hard work they put in to raise us. It is a way of acknowledging the important role they played in shaping who we are today The hormone associated with gratitude is oxytocin. This hormone promotes social bonding and can reduce stress and anxiety levels. Gratitude also fosters a positive outlook, improves sleep quality, and enhances relationships.

As our parents' children, it is our responsibility to ensure that they receive the care and support they need to live comfortably and with dignity. This also sets an example for our own children, teaching them the value of family, respect, and responsibility. By taking care of our parents, we are instilling important values in our children that will serve them well throughout their lives.

However, taking care of aging parents can be a challenging task, especially when trying to balance it with the demands of a married life. While it's important to take care of your parents, it's also important to set boundaries and not let their needs take over your entire life. Have discussions with your partner and your parents about what is realistic and sustainable for everyone involved. Start planning for your parents' care as early as possible. This could include hiring a caregiver, arranging for home modifications, etc.

The Need to Develop Good Habits in the Family

Developing good habits requires a combination of mindset, environment, and behaviour changes. Once this is achieved, it automatically creates a healthy family atmosphere.

Our beliefs and attitudes have a significant impact on our behaviour and actions. If you want to develop good habits, you need to start by changing your belief system. This means identifying any limiting beliefs or negative self-talk that might be holding you back and replacing it with positive affirmations and beliefs that support your goals.

- Old belief: 'I'm not good at communicating with my family.'
- New belief: 'I am capable of improving my communication skills and creating stronger relationships with my family members.'

Your environment and the systems you have in place can also have a significant impact on your habits. If you want to develop good habits, you need to create an environment that supports your goals and helps you stay on track. This might involve decluttering your space, creating a routine that supports your habits, or changing your social circle to surround yourself with people who support and encourage your positive changes.

- Old environment: You want to exercise more, but your home is cluttered and doesn't have a lot of space to move around in.
- New environment: You declutter your space, create a designated workout area, and hang up motivational posters to inspire you to exercise.

To develop good habits, it is important to set clear goals and define what you want to achieve. This helps provide focus and direction and gives you a sense of purpose and motivation.

- Goal: I want to have closer relationships with my siblings.
- New habit: I will call or text my siblings once a week to catch up and show that I care.

Developing good habits requires self-discipline and willpower. This means learning how to resist temptation, stay focused on your goals, and stay motivated even when the going gets tough. Self-discipline is a skill that can be developed with practice and can help you achieve success in all areas of your life.

- Temptation: You want to eat junk food, even though you're trying to eat healthier.
- Self-discipline: You understand the impact, resist the temptation, and choose a healthier option instead.

Finally, it is important to celebrate your successes and acknowledge your progress. This helps to reinforce your positive habits and build confidence and motivation to continue making positive changes.

By changing your belief system, changing your environment and systems, setting clear goals, building self-discipline, and celebrating your successes, you can create positive habits that help you achieve success and fulfilment in all areas of your life.

Bringing Order to Chaos

Everything in the home should have a designated spot where it belongs. This helps to keep one's home organised and tidy. Get rid of anything that you don't use or need. This will free up space and make it easier to organise the things that you do keep. Example: used clothes may be given to any orphanage on any occasion.

Once you've decluttered, take some time to think about how you use your home. Once you have a good understanding of your needs, you can start to create a system for organising your belongings. Example: keeping separate files for documents related to different matters, like health and wealth, and storing soft copies as well.

For each item, designate a specific place where it will be stored. This could be a drawer, a shelf, a basket, or even a specific spot on the floor for easy access. Get everyone in the family involved in the organising process. This will help create a sense of ownership and responsibility. A well-organised home is more efficient, more inviting, and more relaxing, i.e. free from stress.

Getting Out of One's Comfort Zone

Getting out of your comfort zone in the context of family life is important for personal growth and the development of stronger relationships with your loved ones.

Expressing appreciation for your family members, especially in ways that you may not be habituated to, can help you step out of your comfort zone. This can involve writing a heartfelt note, planning a surprise celebration, or simply expressing gratitude for the small things your family members do for you. Stepping out of your comfort zone also means taking on new responsibilities that you may not be used to. This can include cooking dinner for the family, helping with household chores, or taking care of a family member who needs extra support. It's easy to fall into the routine of doing the same things with your family, but trying out new activities together can bring a sense of excitement and adventure. You can suggest going for a hike, trying a new restaurant, or learning a new hobby together. Avoiding difficult conversations or conflicts can create distance and tension in a family. While it may feel uncomfortable, it's important to address issues and work through disagreements in a respectful and open way. This can lead to deeper understanding and more meaningful connections with your family. Being vulnerable with your family means opening up about your feelings, struggles, and aspirations. It can be uncomfortable to share your innermost thoughts and emotions, but it can also create a greater sense of intimacy and closeness in your relationships.

A Safe Home

A safe home protect one's family from physical harm, one's belongings from theft, and one's peace of mind. If family members become victims of a crime, it can have a significant impact on them, which can take the form of:

- Financial hardship
- Emotional distress
- Fear and anxiety
- Disrupted relationships
- Difficulty sleeping
- Difficulty concentrating
- Post-traumatic stress disorder (PTSD)

S A F E   H O M E

Be aware of your neighbours	**S**	Be aware of your servants, servicemen
Keep your doors locked, even when you're at home	**A**	Install deadbolts on all exterior doors
Consider installing a home security system	**F**	Secure your shed or storage room
Add motion sensor lights around your home	**E**	Trim back trees and shrubs
Be careful what you post on social media like posting vacation plans	**H**	Don't leave valuable in plain sight
Sensitise senior citizen about safety	**O**	Don't advertise about your absence
Be aware of your surroundings	**M**	Don't leave keys in your car
	E	

Enthusiasm at the Workplace and at Home

Enthusiasm is a key quality for success and overall wellness, both in the workplace and at home. It has the following benefits:

- *Increases motivation*. When you are enthusiastic about something, it ignites a fire within you that drives you to take action and pursue your goals with greater focus and energy. This can help you stay motivated and overcome any obstacles or challenges that may arise.

- *Boosts creativity*. Enthusiasm can also spark your creativity and help you generate new ideas and solutions. When you are excited and passionate about something, your mind is more open to exploring new possibilities and taking risks.

- *Improves relationships.* Enthusiasm can be contagious, and when you bring positive energy and enthusiasm to your interactions with others, it can improve your relationships and create a more positive work and home environment.
- *Reduces stress.* When you approach your work and home life with enthusiasm, it can help you stay optimistic and positive, even in challenging situations. This can reduce stress and promote overall well-being.
- *Increases productivity.* Enthusiasm can also increase your productivity by helping you focus on the task at hand and stay engaged in your work or home life. This can lead to greater efficiency and better results.

To cultivate enthusiasm, it's important to identify what excites and motivates you and focus on those things. This may involve setting goals that align with your passions, seeking out new challenges and opportunities for growth or finding ways to inject more fun and creativity into your daily routine. It's also important to maintain a positive attitude and look for opportunities to express gratitude and appreciation for the people and things in your life.

The hormone associated with enthusiasm is dopamine. Dopamine is a neurotransmitter that plays a crucial role in generating feelings of reward and motivation. When we experience something pleasurable or exciting, dopamine is released in the brain, which reinforces the behaviour or activity that led to the pleasurable experience. In terms of enthusiasm, dopamine can help increase one's levels of energy, focus, and engagement. It can also contribute to a sense of pleasure and excitement, which can enhance feelings of enthusiasm.

By cultivating enthusiasm in your work and home life, you can achieve greater fulfilment and success and also create a more positive and rewarding environment for yourself and those around you.

Parenting

The adage **'What doesn't bend at five doesn't bend at fifty'** carries profound wisdom, emphasising the critical role of early intervention and adaptability in the upbringing of children. It signifies that the attitudes, behaviours, and habits forged in a child's formative years possess a remarkable tenacity. It also underscores the formidable challenges entailed in reshaping deeply ingrained aspects of ourselves, highlighting the significance of early intervention and nurturing surroundings while also conveying that effecting change may necessitate sustained dedication and a comprehensive, multi-pronged approach.

These initial stages, often dubbed the 'formative years', constitute a pivotal juncture in a child's holistic development. Within this span, children undergo substantial strides in the physical, cognitive, emotional, and social realms. The burgeoning brain experiences a rapid surge in growth, laying the bedrock for future learning, behaviour, and overall well-being.

Crucially, interactions with parents and caregivers wield a profound influence in sculpting a child's social and emotional landscape, imparting invaluable lessons about emotions, empathy, and the art of forming nurturing relationships. Moreover, this phase is an opportune period for linguistic blossoming, during which children voraciously absorb and assimilate language from their surroundings. The establishment of healthful routines encompassing sleep, nutrition, hygiene, and physical activity assumes paramount importance.

Providing children with a secure and nurturing environment empowers them to embark on explorations, cultivating a burgeoning sense of autonomy that, in turn, fosters the growth of confidence and a robust self-identity. Parents assume the pivotal role of custodians in passing down cultural, moral, and ethical values, thereby shaping the ethical compass of their offspring. Recognising and proactively addressing any potential developmental hurdles or delays in these nascent stages is of paramount importance. With the decline of the joint family system and its implications on child care, parents must be extra vigilant during these golden years.

In essence, the early years provide parents with opportunities to wield a profound influence on their child's development. Active involvement, alongside the provision of a nurturing environment and judiciously tailored stimuli and guidance, can reverberate with a transformative resonance, leaving an indelible mark on a child's overall well-being and future trajectory.

Due to a lack of awareness or understanding, **some parents might be hesitant to allow their children to experience age-appropriate challenges**. Some parents may have an overprotective nature, leading them to constantly fear that their child may get hurt physically or emotionally. They might shield their children from challenges, thinking it will keep them safe and happy. However, excessive protection can hinder a child's emotional growth and prevent them from developing important life skills. Parents might compare their children to others or have high expectations of them. In an attempt to create a smooth path for their children, they may inadvertently shield them from challenges. This could be driven by a desire for their children to achieve more or avoid any perceived failures. Cultural norms and societal pressures can influence parenting styles. Consequently, they might avoid allowing their children to face challenges that could interfere with their achievements. Some parents may have anxieties and unresolved emotional issues, which could make them reluctant to expose their children to potential challenges. They might project their fears onto their children, inadvertently limiting their experiences. Some parents may not fully understand the benefits of age-appropriate challenges or how they contribute to their child's emotional development. They might not realise that shielding children from challenges can hinder their growth. In today's fast-paced world, parents might face time constraints and high levels of stress. As a result, they may find it easier to resolve their children's challenges or make decisions for them rather than allowing them to learn from experience.

Parenting workshops, educational resources, and support groups can provide valuable information and help parents gain a better understanding of child development.

Parenting is a continuous learning process, and promoting awareness of age-appropriate challenges can create a positive and nurturing environment for children to grow into emotionally healthy and resilient adults.

Being a parent is a challenging and rewarding responsibility. Every parent wants their child to grow up to be successful and happy. While there is no one-size-fits-all approach to parenting, there are certain qualities and practices that parents can cultivate to help their children become holistic individuals:

- *Encourage a balanced lifestyle*. Children need a balance of physical activity, intellectual stimulation, social interaction, and rest. Parents can provide opportunities for their children to engage in a variety of activities and help them prioritise how they use their time to make them holistic individuals.
- *Provide love and affection*. A loving and affectionate environment is crucial for a child's emotional and psychological development. Parents who express love and affection to their children through physical touch and positive words and actions help foster a sense of security and self-worth in their children.
- *Provide support and encouragement*. Children need their parents to support and encourage them in their endeavours, whether in academics, sports, or other activities. Parents who provide positive reinforcement and help their children build confidence and resilience can help them develop a strong sense of self-belief and the motivation to pursue their goals.
- *Empathy and listening skills*. Empathetic and attentive parents who listen to their children and understand their feelings and emotions create an environment that fosters healthy communication. This helps children develop their emotional intelligence. Children who understand and value the feelings and perspectives of others are more likely to develop positive relationships and succeed in social situations.
- *Talk to your children about their feelings*. Let them know that it's okay to feel sad, angry, or scared. Help them learn how to cope with their emotions in a healthy way.
- *Spend quality time with your children*. This shows them that you love and care about them. It also gives you a chance to get to know them better and to help them develop their interests.
- *Provide consistency and structure*. Establishing clear boundaries, routines, and expectations helps children feel secure and develop a sense of responsibility. Parents who provide structure and consistency to their children's lives help them learn self-discipline and organisation, which are crucial skills for success in adulthood.
- *Be role models*. Parents who lead by example and demonstrate positive behaviours and values instil those same qualities in their children. Children

learn from watching their parents' actions, so it is important to exhibit the qualities and behaviours that parents hope to see in their children.

- *Encourage independence.* Children who are allowed to make choices and decisions appropriate to their age and maturity level are more likely to develop self-confidence and independence. Parents can encourage independence by providing age-appropriate responsibilities and allowing their children to make choices within safe boundaries.

- *Develop a strong sense of self-worth.* Children need to feel good about themselves in order to thrive. Parents can help them develop a strong sense of self-worth by praising their accomplishments, providing them with positive feedback, and teaching them to value themselves for who they are.

By fostering a growth mindset, empathy, and independence, parents can provide their children with the tools they need to succeed in all areas of life.

Nature's Extraordinary Parenting Approaches

In today's fast-paced world, while parents strive to offer the best upbringing to their children, there can sometimes be inadvertent lapses in understanding the holistic development needed. In the wondrous realm of nature, birds and animals exhibit remarkable parenting approaches to ensure the development of their offspring. They begin with a period of devoted care, equipping their young ones with essential survival skills and knowledge of the environment.

As time progresses, these exceptional creatures transition into a more demanding parenting style. They expose their young to challenging situations, allowing them to face life's trials independently. This fosters resilience, adaptability, and resourcefulness, crucial for thriving in the wild.

- Eagle parents, renowned for their aerial prowess, engage in a captivating dance with their fledglings, encouraging flight. This daring teaching method strengthens flying abilities and ignites courage within the young eagles, empowering them to soar higher.

- Similarly, majestic elephant mothers employ a compassionate yet tough approach. They teach their calves navigation and survival skills, fostering problem-solving abilities. Through independence, young elephants develop self-reliance and confidence.

- Female sea turtles lay eggs on sandy beaches and leave the hatchlings to navigate to the ocean. This arduous journey tests survival instincts, preparing the young turtles for life at sea.

- Within the beehive, worker bees construct hexagonal honeycomb cells, nurturing their larvae into fully developed adult bees. Each bee assumes diverse roles, contributing to the hive's well-being.
- In the frigid Antarctic, emperor penguins endure harsh conditions while raising chicks. As the chicks grow, the parents gradually reduce assistance, encouraging independence and group behaviour, which are both essential for survival.
- Cheetah mothers impart hunting skills to their cubs, allowing them to participate in hunts gradually. This process ensures the young cheetahs become skilled hunters, sustaining themselves in the competitive savannah.

Drawing inspiration from these insights, modern parents can create an atmosphere that nurtures emotional intelligence, resilience, and self-assurance in their children. Guided by the wisdom of nature, they can inspire independence, establish healthy boundaries, provide attentive support, and cultivate empathy, exploration, and creativity. By embracing these invaluable life lessons, parents enrich their children's lives and promote remarkable growth and well-being.

The Impact of Negligence on the Physical-emotional Health of Kids

Many parents may fail to unlock the full potential of their children due to the lack of a holistic approach. They have to recognise that their children's potential is not just limited to their academic abilities. Instead, they must focus on developing their children's physical health, emotional well-being, social skills, and intellectual curiosity, which give exposure to a range of experiences and activities that help them develop their interests and passions. A few things to note in this regard:

- Parents who don't encourage their children to engage in physical activity or who discourage them from participating in sports and other types of exercise can put their children's health at risk.
- Many parents may be unaware of the importance of protein in their children's diet and may therefore fail to provide them with enough protein-rich foods such as lean meats like chicken and fish, eggs, dairy products, legumes, nuts, and seeds. Some parents may omit to include fruits, vegetables, and other nutritious foods in their children's diets. Parents who skip meals and regularly offer their children unhealthy foods, such as fast food or sugary snacks, can put their children's health at risk. Doing so after exercise can undermine the benefits of the workout and contribute to poor health outcomes.

- Allowing children to spend too much time in front of television, phone, or computer screens can be harmful to a child's physical and mental health.
- Children need adequate sleep to support their physical and mental health, so failing to enforce regular bedtime routines can be harmful.
- Children can become sick or injured quickly, and it's important for parents to pay attention to any signs of illness or injury and seek medical attention when necessary.

It's important to make parents aware of the importance of healthy behaviours and the potential risks of unhealthy habits.

Understanding the Behaviour of 'Spoilt' Kids

Spoilt kids often have an entitled attitude, believing that they are entitled to have whatever they want, whenever they want it, without having to work for it. They tend to lack empathy, independence, and resilience, have poor social skills, practise disrespectful behaviour, and be unable to delay gratification.

Causes

Parents who excessively pamper or indulge their children may inadvertently encourage spoilt behaviour by reinforcing the idea that their child deserves to have whatever they want whenever they want it. The following parenting practices can lead to spoilt behaviour:

- Not setting clear boundaries.
- Not holding children accountable for their bad behaviour or teaching them that their actions have consequences.
- Not enforcing consistent discipline.
- Giving children too many material possessions.
- Indulging children due to stress or out of guilt over one's parenting mistakes.

Children who experience the above parenting behaviours may lack empathy for others, develop a sense of entitlement and an unhealthy attachment to material goods, and exhibit spoilt behaviour.

Correcting Spoilt Behaviour

- Spoilt kids may spend a lot of time indoors engaging in sedentary activities, so parents can encourage them to participate in physical activities by providing opportunities for outdoor play, sports, etc.

- These kids may have unhealthy eating habits, so parents can encourage healthy eating habits by providing nutritious meals and snacks and limiting unhealthy options.

- These kids may lack independence, so parents can encourage independence by giving their children opportunities to make decisions and solve problems on their own. This can help build their self-confidence and self-esteem.

- They may not understand or respect boundaries, so it's important for parents to set clear and consistent limits on their behaviour. This includes setting rules for behaviour and consequences for breaking rules and enforcing these boundaries consistently.

In the Indian Constitution, while fundamental freedoms are guaranteed to citizens, these rights are subject to reasonable restrictions in the interests of public order, morality, health, and the general welfare of society. This balance between individual freedoms and societal well-being is crucial to maintaining harmony and preventing the misuse of rights. Parenting also involves a similar balance between granting children a certain degree of freedom while setting appropriate boundaries for their well-rounded development. **Just as the Constitution recognises both individual rights and the need for restrictions, parents must allow children to explore, learn, and make choices, while also providing guidance and limitations to ensure their safety, values, and overall growth.** This approach helps children develop independence, responsibility, and a strong moral compass within the framework of a supportive and nurturing environment.

Equipping Children with Self-awareness Skills

According to the World Health Organization (WHO), approximately one billion children aged 2–17 years (or half of all children in the world) have experienced physical, sexual, or emotional violence or neglect in the past year. According to the United Nations Office on Drugs and Crime, children make up almost a third of all human trafficking victims worldwide, with girls being particularly vulnerable to sexual exploitation.

Hence, children are highly vulnerable to crime in our society. It is important for parents and caregivers to teach children self-awareness skills to help them stay safe and avoid dangerous situations.

- *Teach children to recognise warning signs/threats*. Children should be taught to recognise warning signs that indicate danger, such as being followed, being approached by strangers, or feeling uncomfortable in a situation.
- *Develop assertiveness*. Children should be taught to be assertive and stand up for themselves. This includes saying 'no' when they are uncomfortable or threatened and asking for help when they need it.
- *Practise situational awareness*. Children should be taught to be aware of their surroundings and pay attention to what is happening around them. They should also be taught to trust their instincts and exit a situation if they feel uncomfortable or unsafe.
- *Encourage open communication*. Encourage children to talk openly and honestly about their experiences and feelings. This includes discussing any concerns or fears they may have about their safety.
- *Establish clear boundaries*. Children should be taught to establish clear boundaries with others. This includes setting limits on physical contact and personal space and avoiding situations that make them uncomfortable.
- *Develop problem-solving skills*. Children should be taught problem-solving skills to help them handle challenging situations. This includes identifying options, weighing pros and cons, and making informed decisions.
- *Internet safety*. Children should be taught to be aware of the risks associated with the internet and social media. Scammers and phishes are always looking for ways to steal personal information and one must be careful about clicking on links to websites that one is not familiar with.
- *Knowing emergency procedures*. Children should be taught what to do in emergency situations—how to call for help, what to do if they are lost, and how to get to a safe place. Children should know how to dial emergency numbers.

Adolescents and Social Media

Adolescents need to be made aware of the risks associated with social media, including cyberbullying, identity theft, and online predators.

- Parents should have an open and honest conversation with their children about these risks and how to avoid them. Adolescents should be encouraged to communicate openly and honestly with their parents about their online experiences, and parents should be approachable and non-judgmental so that their children feel comfortable sharing their concerns.

- Adolescents should be taught to think critically about the information and online friends they encounter on social media. They should be encouraged to question the validity of sources and to fact-check information before sharing it.

- Parents should set clear boundaries on their children's use of social media, including time limits and restrictions on access to certain apps or websites.

- Parents should monitor their children's online activity, including their social media accounts, to ensure their safety. Parents should be aware of the apps and websites their children are using and should have access to their accounts.

- Adolescents should be taught to behave responsibly online, which includes avoiding cyberbullying, not sharing personal information, and being respectful to others. Parents should be role models of responsible online behaviour themselves.

Seeing is Greater than Hearing

Seeing is often more powerful than hearing when it comes to learning and behaviour, and this can have important implications for children who are learning from their parents and other role models.

When we see something, our brains process that information in a more direct and immediate way than when we simply hear about it. This is because our visual sense is highly developed and our brains are wired to prioritise visual information over other types of sensory information.

When children see their parents or other role models engaging in certain behaviours, they are more likely to imitate those behaviours themselves. This is because they are able to see the behaviour in action and understand exactly how it is done, rather than simply hearing about it and having to imagine what it might look like. For example, if a child sees their parent consistently practising healthy eating habits and engaging in regular exercise, they are more likely to develop those same habits themselves. Similarly, if a child sees their parent consistently engaging in positive social behaviours, such as being kind to others and resolving conflicts in a respectful manner, they are more likely to develop those same behaviours themselves. On the other hand, if a child sees their parent engaging in negative behaviours, such as being aggressive or using drugs or alcohol, they are more likely to develop those same behaviours themselves. When you point a finger at your child, four fingers are pointing back at you. It is a reflection of your parenting, not solely your child's mistake.

Overall, the power of visual learning and observation is an important consideration for parents and other role models who are trying to set a positive example for children. By demonstrating positive behaviours and attitudes and by being mindful of what they are conveying through their actions and words, parents can help ensure that their children learn and grow in healthy and positive ways.

Development of Learning and Listening skills

Developing a love of learning and listening in children is important for their academic and personal growth.

Children have different learning styles, so it's important to use a variety of teaching methods to keep them engaged and interested in learning. This can include visual aids, hands-on activities, and online resources. Parents can foster a love of learning by encouraging their children to explore their interests and passions. This can involve providing opportunities for children to pursue their hobbies or participate in extracurricular activities that align with their interests. Encourage children to engage in active learning by asking questions, participating in discussions, and using hands-on learning techniques.

Time management skills are essential for effective studying. Parents can teach children how to manage their time effectively by setting schedules, prioritising tasks, and avoiding distractions. Children are more likely to enjoy studying when they have a positive and supportive learning environment. This can include having a designated study space, a quiet and organised workspace, and access to necessary learning materials.

Positive reinforcement can be used to encourage children to continue learning and exploring new things. Parents can provide praise and rewards for good listening habits, such as paying attention, responding appropriately, and following directions. Active listening skills involve paying attention, summarising what was said, and asking follow-up questions. As children learn by observing and mimicking the behaviours of their parents or caregivers, parents should exhibit good listening skills by maintaining eye contact, focusing on what the child is saying, and responding appropriately. Eliminate distractions such as loud music, TV, or other background noise when the child is trying to listen. Ensure that the child has a comfortable and quiet environment for studying, learning, or listening.

Cultivating Brilliance: Nurturing Your Child's Unique Abilities

Discovering a child's unique abilities is like embarking on a captivating journey of exploration and growth. Just as an artist's brush strokes reveal their masterpiece, observing a child's behaviour and reactions unveils the canvas of their passions. Getting children to engage in a variety of activities, from arts and crafts to culinary adventures, will help them discover their innate talents. Through open dialogues that mirror the purest reflections of their thoughts, children reveal the colours of their aspirations. Parents can view themselves as guardians of inspiration, tasked with introducing their children to a kaleidoscope of experiences that will enable them to dance to the melody of possibility. Every puzzle solved, every challenge met, becomes a stone in the mosaic of their unique abilities. Encouragement and support breathe life into their endeavours, nurturing the blossoming of their gifts. With patience as a guiding star, this odyssey of self-discovery unfolds organically, allowing a child to compose their own masterpiece of talent and passion, one brush stroke at a time.

Parental Roles in Nurturing Athletic Potential: A Balanced Approach

Parents can play various roles in nurturing their child's athletic potential, such as providing emotional support, financial resources, and encouragement. Introducing children to a wide range of sports and physical activities from an early age allows them to experience different movements, skills, and environments. This exposure helps them discover what sports they enjoy and excel at. Some may have exceptional speed, agility, hand-eye coordination, or endurance, which can hint at their potential in specific sports. Once potential talents are identified, parents can provide opportunities for skill development. Enrolling children in classes, camps, or clubs related to their interests will help them refine their skills. Children's interests can evolve over time. Parents should be flexible and supportive if their child's athletic pursuits change or evolve as they grow older. While supporting their child's aspirations, parents should strike a balance between academics and sports. **Parents should not impose their unfulfilled dreams on their children. It's crucial for parents not to focus too much on winning. The emphasis should be on personal growth, skill development, and enjoyment of the sport.** Parents should provide emotional support and create a positive environment. Encouraging resilience, discipline, and good sportsmanship is vital, for these are the qualities that will help the child navigate the challenges of competitive sports and handle setbacks and failures. Intense training regimes and competitive pressure can lead to burnout and physical or mental exhaustion. It's essential to recognise and respect the child's individual aspirations and desires. In the pursuit of excellence, some parents may be tempted to bend rules or push their child beyond their limits. Ensuring ethical behaviour and fair play should always be prioritised. By actively exploring their children's athletic talents, parents can help them discover their passions and potential in sports, leading to a positive and fulfilling sports experience.

Holistic Home Management

Holistic home maintenance is a comprehensive approach to caring for your home that considers all aspects of its well-being. It is about taking proactive measures to care for your living space. It's not just about fixing problems when they arise, but also about preventing them and optimising your home for longevity, comfort, and value.

In the living room, cultivate a warm and welcoming atmosphere with comfortable seating, soft lighting, and personal touches like family photos or artwork. Encourage family time and consider incorporating a small library to promote reading and lifelong learning. The living room is also a space for hospitality; it's where guests are often welcomed. Ensure that there's ample seating and a layout that facilitates conversation. Avoid using the living room as a workspace or storage area for unused items. Maintain a clean and clutter-free space and opt for gentle lighting to create a peaceful ambiance. By prioritising both family bonding and a hospitability, you can make the living room a central hub for meaningful interactions and warm welcomes.

In the bedroom, it's essential to create an inviting atmosphere with soothing colours and personal touches. Use comfortable bedding, start each day by making the bed, and keep the space tidy and well-organised. Setting a regular sleep schedule and avoiding electronic devices in bed helps ensure quality rest. Steer clear of clutter, bright colours, and work-related items, and reserve the bedroom solely for sleep and intimacy, not for activities like eating or excessive screen time.

The kitchen should be a haven of cleanliness and hygiene. Additionally, avoid using plastic containers for food storage and opt for eco-friendly cleaning products to maintain a safe and healthy kitchen environment.

For the bathroom, prioritise cleanliness and ventilation. Use natural, eco-friendly cleaning products and ensure essential toiletries are readily available. Create a calming atmosphere with scented candles or essential oils, and promote proper hygiene habits, especially hand washing. Avoid using harsh chemicals that could harm the environment or skin, steer clear of clutter, and avoid excessive grooming or makeup application in the bathroom.

A fitness room in your home can be a wonderful addition for the promotion of an active lifestyle. Keep the space clear of obstacles or clutter that could pose risks during physical activity. Invest in quality exercise equipment that aligns with your fitness goals. To stay motivated, add elements like motivational quotes, a sound system for music, or even a TV. Ensure safety with proper lighting, covered outlets, and a first-aid kit for emergencies. Additionally, consider designating a corner for meditation or mindfulness practices, providing a serene space for mental wellness. Choose non-slip flooring, prioritise ventilation, follow safety measures like warming up before exercise, and maintain hygiene by regularly cleaning equipment and surfaces. By incorporating meditation into your fitness room, you can create a holistic environment that nurtures both physical and mental well-being.

Additionally, consider energy-efficient upgrades, landscaping, and keeping up with interior and exterior design trends. Taking this comprehensive approach can lead to a home that not only retains its value but also provides a safe and comfortable living environment for all family members.

Hygiene at Home

Bacteria and other pathogens that cause illnesses and infections tend to proliferate in specific areas within homes, particularly areas, surfaces and objects that are exposed to moisture, warmth, and the accumulation of organic matter. These hotspots include kitchen sponges, sinks, and cutting boards, where food residue gathers, and bathroom towels and toothbrush holders, which stay damp. High-touch surfaces such as doorknobs, light switches, and remotes also harbour bacteria from our hands. Pet bowls, refrigerator seals, and garbage cans accumulate moisture and organic waste, attracting bacteria. Carpets and rugs can trap moisture, turning into breeding grounds. To prevent bacterial growth and maintain a hygienic living environment, regular cleaning, disinfecting, and proper ventilation are essential.

Hygiene Hypothesis

Exposure to certain types of pollutants, such as lead and mercury, can actually have harmful effects on the immune system, as can exposure to certain types of bacteria and viruses that can cause serious illnesses and infections.

Ironically, there is some evidence to suggest that exposure to certain types of pollution and unhygienic conditions can help stimulate and strengthen the immune system. This is known as the 'hygiene hypothesis'. The idea behind the hygiene hypothesis is that exposure to a range of different germs and bacteria during childhood can help the immune system develop more robustly and effectively. This is because exposure to germs and bacteria helps 'train' the immune system to recognise and respond to a range of different pathogens, which can improve its ability to fight off infections and illnesses. There is also evidence to suggest that exposure to certain types of pollution, such as airborne particles and toxins, can have a similar effect on the immune system. While exposure to certain types of pollution and unhygienic conditions may help stimulate and strengthen the immune system, it's important to be cautious and avoid exposure to harmful pollutants and pathogens by maintaining good hygiene practices.

Checklist for Couples

Emotional Expression
- Do you recognise that men and women may express emotions differently, and are you attentive to your partner's emotional needs and expressions?

Conflict Resolution
- Are you aware that men and women may approach conflict resolution differently, with some men tending to withdraw and women seeking to discuss issues openly, and do you make an effort to find a middle ground that works for both of you?
- Do you find yourself silently offering forgiveness to your partner while patiently awaiting improved circumstances?

Supportive Roles
- Have you discussed and agreed upon the roles and responsibilities in your relationship, understanding that these roles may differ from traditional gender norms?

Individual Preferences
- Are you attuned to your partner's individual preferences and needs, recognising that these may not align perfectly with stereotypical gender expectations?

Empathy and Understanding
- Do you actively practise empathy and understanding when it comes to your partner's experiences and perspectives as a person of a different gender?

Open Communication

- Do you prioritise open and honest communication in your relationship?

Quality Time Together

- Do you set aside quality time for each other without distractions?

Shared Goals

- Have you established common short-term and long-term goals together?

Individual Growth

- Do you give each other space for personal growth and individual pursuits?

Financial Goals

- Have you created a budget and discussed financial goals?

Respect and Appreciation

- Do you show respect and express appreciation for each other?

Emotional Support

- Are you there for each other during difficult times?

Physical Intimacy

- Do you maintain a healthy physical connection in your relationship?

Shared Responsibilities

- Do you and your partner divide household responsibilities in a way that feels fair to both of you?

Trust and Reliability

- Do you trust each other and keep promises?

Continuous Learning

- Do you invest in learning and growing together as a couple?

Health Support

- Do you support each other's health and wellness goals?

Celebrating Milestones

- Do you acknowledge and celebrate achievements and milestones?

Shared Activities
- Do you have shared hobbies or activities that you enjoy together?

Adaptability
- Are you both willing to adapt to changes and challenges in your lives?

In-Law Relationships
- Do you maintain positive and respectful relationships with each other's families?

Eating Meals Together
- Do you make an effort to have regular meals together as a couple?

Expressing Love and Affection
- Do you regularly express love and affection for each other?

Taking Care of Parents-in-law
- Do you take sufficient care of your parents-in-law, at least as a token of gratitude?

Comprehensive Checklist (Quarterly)for Ideal Parenting

Emotional Connection
- Have you maintained a strong emotional connection with your child?
- Do you regularly engage in open and honest conversations with your child about their feelings and emotions?

Emotional Support
- Have you been a reliable source of emotional support for your child during challenges and achievements?
- Have you encouraged resilience and coping skills?

Emotional Regulation
- Have you helped your child develop emotional regulation skills to manage their emotions effectively?
- Have you provided a safe space for your child to express their feelings without judgment?

Quality Time

- Do you engage in creative activities with your kids?
- Have you spent quality one-on-one time with your child, engaging in activities they enjoy?
- Have you participated in family activities and bonding experiences?

Communication

- Have you practised effective and respectful communication with your child?
- Do you actively listen to your child's thoughts and concerns without judgment?

Setting Boundaries

- Have you established clear and age-appropriate boundaries for your child?
- Have you consistently enforced these boundaries while being firm yet nurturing?

Discipline

- Have you used positive disciplining techniques to guide your child's behaviour?
- Do you provide explanations and opportunities to help your child learn from mistakes?

Education and Learning

- Have you supported your child's educational journey?
- Have you encouraged a love for learning and exploration?

Health and Well-being

- Have you ensured your child's physical health?
- Have you promoted healthy eating habits and encouraged physical activity?

Social Skills

- Have you provided opportunities for your child to develop social skills and interact with peers?
- Have you addressed any social challenges your child may be facing?

Independence and Responsibility

- Have you encouraged age-appropriate independence and responsibility?
- Have you involved your child in household chores and decision-making?

Hobbies and Interests

- Have you supported and nurtured your child's hobbies and interests?
- Have you provided opportunities for skill development and the exploration of new interests?

Safety and Security

- Have you ensured a safe and secure environment for your child at home and outside?
- Have you educated your child about safety measures and potential risks?

Encouragement and Motivation

- Have you offered praise and encouragement for your child's efforts and achievements?
- Have you motivated your child to set and pursue their goals?

Empathy and Understanding

- Have you demonstrated empathy and understanding in your interactions with others?
- Have you taught your child to be empathetic and compassionate towards others?

Screen Time Management

- Have you monitored and managed your child's screen time and digital activities?
- Have you encouraged a healthy balance between their use of technology and other activities?

Cultural and Moral Values

- Have you shared and upheld your family's cultural and moral values with your child?
- Have you taught them about tolerance, respect, and inclusivity?

Self-Care

- Have you practised self-care and management of your own stress and emotions effectively?
- Have you demonstrated the importance of self-care to your child?

Parental Growth and Learning

- Have you sought opportunities for personal growth and learning as a parent?
- Have you adapted your parenting strategies based on new knowledge and insights?

Conflict Resolution

- Have you taught your child healthy ways to resolve conflicts with others?
- Have you demonstrated effective conflict resolution in your interactions with family members and others?

Diversity and Inclusion

- Have you exposed your child to diverse cultures, beliefs, and perspectives?
- Have you discussed the importance of inclusivity and respecting differences?

Limiting Screen Time

- Have you set clear limits on screen time?
- Have you encouraged alternative activities that promote creativity and physical activity?

Financial Literacy

- Have you started teaching your child age-appropriate financial concepts, such as saving and budgeting?
- Have you encouraged them to make responsible financial decisions?

Healthy Sleep Habits

- Have you established a consistent sleep routine that promotes healthy sleep habits?
- Have you ensured your child is getting sufficient rest based on their age?

Personal Hygiene and Health

- Have you taught your child about personal hygiene practices, such as handwashing and dental care?
- Have you discussed the importance of maintaining overall health and seeking medical attention when needed?

Media Literacy and Critical Thinking

- Have you helped your child develop media literacy skills to analyse and question the information they encounter?
- Have you encouraged critical thinking and discernment in their media consumption?

Respecting Privacy and Boundaries

- Have you taught your child about respecting others' privacy and personal boundaries?
- Have you discussed the importance of seeking consent in their interactions with others?

Gratitude and Appreciation

- Have you encouraged your child to express gratitude and appreciation for the people and things in their life?
- Have you demonstrated gratitude in your daily interactions?

Environmental Consciousness

- Have you educated your child about the importance of environmental conservation and sustainable practices?
- Have you involved them in activities that promote eco-friendly habits?

Future Planning and Goal-Setting

- Have you discussed future plans and goals with your child, encouraging them to envision their aspirations?
- Have you supported them in setting achievable short-term and long-term goals?

Checklist for Youngsters (After Completion of Studies)

Self-discovery

- Have you taken the time to reflect on your passions, values, interests, and plans by creating self-discuss lists?
- Do you have a deep understanding of your natural strengths and weaknesses, such as willpower, resilience, creativity, adaptability?
- Do you follow the crowd or do you forge your own path?
- Do you cultivate an insatiable hunger for success to reach your maximum potential?
- Do you understand the differences between the permanent and temporary things in life, such as immature relationships?
- Are you aware that, by being mindful of our actions, attitudes, and decisions today, we can consciously create a desirable future?
- Have you noticed a paradigm shift in the use of gadgets, transitioning from leisure to productivity?
- Do you seek opinions from your trusted ones if you are confused about your strengths and weaknesses?

Personal Growth

- Are you committed to your personal growth and development?
- Do you absorb everything you can to become a maestro in your craft?
- Are you open to new experiences and challenges?
- Are you willing to learn from your mistakes?
- Are you cultivating the habit of resilience or are you expecting instant success?
- Do you have the ability to identify time-wasting routines and instances of time loss in a day?
- Have you identified potential productivity obstacles/distractions?
- Do you dive into a language that you are trying to learn by listening to podcasts and using learning apps every day?
- Do you take steps to do the things that scare you, like public speaking?
- Do you improve your posture, body language, facial expression, hairstyle, and dressing sense to take pride in your appearance?

Professional Development

- Are you committed to lifelong learning and staying updated in your field?
- Do you follow any techniques like kaizen or shoshin(beginner's mind) to beat laziness?
- Have you considered attending workshops, conferences, or online courses?

Career Goals

- Have you defined your career goals and aspirations?

Job Search

- Have you started actively searching for job opportunities in your field of interest?
- Do you have a well-prepared resume and cover letter?

Skill Development

- Are there any additional skills or certifications you need to enhance your employability?
- Are you considering further education or specialised training?

Stress Management

- Do you have strategies in place for managing stress effectively?
- Are you aware of the mental health resources and support available to you?
- Do you have effective time/mind management strategies to balance work, hobbies, and your goals?

Health and Wellness

- Are you aware that poor health habits can lead to serious health problems later in life?
- Are you taking care of your physical and mental health?
- Do you have a regular exercise routine and a balanced diet?

Networking

- Have you been networking with professionals in your industry?
- Are you building relationships that can help your career?

Friendships

- Are you maintaining and nurturing your healthy friendships?
- Do you have a support network of friends?

Cultural and Social Awareness
- Are you aware of and respectful of cultural and social diversity?
- Are you educating yourself about global issues and current events?

Financial Literacy
- Do you have a basic understanding of personal finance?
- Do you avoid spending too much money on unnecessary things and taking on too much debt?
- Do you have a plan for your financial future?

Housing Options
- Have you thought about where you want to live and have you explored different housing options (renting, buying)?
- Do you have a plan for finding suitable accommodation?

Legal Responsibilities
- Are you aware of your legal responsibilities, such as taxes and local laws?
- Do you understand your rights and obligations as a citizen or resident?

Charitable Contributions
- Have you thought about how you can give back to society or support charitable causes for your personal satisfaction?
- Are you planning to allocate a portion of your income or time to philanthropic activities?

Online Presence
- Have you reviewed and adjusted your online presence (social media, professional profiles) for potential employers or partners to see?
- Are you mindful of your digital footprint and its impact on your personal and professional life?

Marriage Planning
- Have you considered when and where you'd like to get married?
- Have you thought about the size and style of your wedding?
- Have you set important life goals and values that need to be discussed with your partner?

Healthy Society

A healthy society is a community or a population that demonstrates overall well-being, both physically and mentally. Health in this context encompasses various aspects of life, including individuals' physical health, emotional and mental well-being, social connections, and the overall quality of life.

A healthy society is one in which all members have the opportunity to live long, healthy, and fulfilling lives and access to quality healthcare, education, employment, and a safe and supportive environment.

Culture plays a significant role in shaping and influencing a healthy society. It consists of the shared beliefs, values, customs, traditions, and behaviours of a group of people. Cultural beliefs about health and well-being influence the dissemination and understanding of health information and can influence individuals' behaviours and choices related to healthcare. For example, some cultures prioritise proactive measures such as regular physical activity and balanced diets, while others may have traditional healing practices or herbal remedies. These beliefs can influence health-seeking behaviours, adherence to medical treatments, and overall health outcomes. Similarly, cultural attitudes towards physical activity, nutrition, substance use, and sexual health can impact the prevalence of healthy or unhealthy behaviours within a society and cultural norms that discourage smoking and risky sexual behaviours contribute to a healthier society overall. Food preferences and dietary habits are strongly influenced by culture. Different cultures have unique culinary traditions, ingredients, and cooking techniques. These factors shape people's eating habits, which in turn impact their overall health. For example, cultures that traditionally consume a balanced diet rich in fruits, vegetables, and whole grains tend to have lower rates of diet-related diseases such as obesity, diabetes, and cardiovascular disorders.

Cultures that promote understanding, acceptance, and support for mental health can contribute to a healthier society by reducing stigma and facilitating access to mental health services. Strong social networks and support systems provide individuals with emotional, instrumental, and informational support, which can positively influence physical and mental well-being. Cultural celebrations, gatherings, and community activities can foster a sense of belonging and social integration, promoting overall health and happiness.

It is important to note that culture is not static and evolves over time. A healthy society recognises the need for cultural diversity, adaptation, and dialogue between different cultural groups. Culture can be a catalyst for social change and advocacy. For example, the concept of kaizen, which has its origins in post-World War II Japan, when the country was focused on rebuilding its economy, has become deeply ingrained in Japanese culture and finds application in various aspects of Japanese society. The philosophy was embraced by companies like Toyota, which sought to enhance productivity and quality. Over time, this mindset permeated various aspects of Japanese society and became a cultural norm. Kaizen requires consistent effort and attention to detail, encourages individuals to believe in their capacity for improvement and thereby promotes a growth mindset, and emphasises taking small, manageable steps toward a larger goal and achieving balance in life through the assessment and adjustment of priorities by individuals and the appropriate allocation of time and energy to different areas, such as work, relationships, personal growth, and self-care. Kaizen is not only seen as a management tool but also as a way of life that promotes continuous improvement and contributes to the overall well-being and success of individuals and society as a whole.

Social Impact of the Negative Emotions of Individuals

The negative emotions of individuals can have several critical impacts on society. These emotions, when left unaddressed or uncontrolled, can create a ripple effect that influences the collective behaviour and well-being of a community.

Negative emotions like anger, hatred, and sudden provocation can lead to interpersonal conflicts within society. These conflicts can manifest in various forms, such as verbal altercations, physical violence, or even larger-scale confrontations like riots and protests. Prolonged social conflicts can result in divisions within communities, hindering cooperation and unity. When individuals experience negative emotions like jealousy, greed, or betrayal, it can erode trust in relationships and institutions. In society, a lack of trust can lead to a breakdown in social bonds, scepticism towards authority, and reduced willingness to cooperate, making it challenging to address collective problems effectively. High levels of anxiety, depression, and stress in individuals can collectively impact the mental health of society. A society with widespread mental health issues and drug abuse may experience reduced productivity, increased healthcare costs, and diminished overall well-being.

Negative emotions like jealousy, envy, and resentment can lead to social isolation, as individuals may withdraw from social interactions due to feelings of inadequacy or fear of judgment. Negative emotions, such as greed and avarice, can influence economic behaviour, leading to unethical business practices, financial fraud, and corruption. These actions can harm the economy and exacerbate income inequality within society. Negative emotions can shape cultural norms and social behaviours. For example, a society where aggression is celebrated or normalised may perpetuate a cycle of violence and hostility, impacting the well-being of its members. Negative emotions can fuel prejudice and discrimination towards certain groups or individuals. Jealousy or fear of others' success or differences can lead to discriminatory attitudes, perpetuating social injustices and inequality. Emotions can be contagious, and negative emotions can spread rapidly within a society. For example, fear and panic during a crisis can lead to mass hysteria and irrational behaviour, impacting public safety and emergency responses.

Negative emotions, such as anger, lust, jealousy, greed, and anxiety, can have significant effects on individuals, leading to emotional turmoil, strained relationships, and compromised mental health. When these emotions become pervasive in society, they contribute to a toxic social environment marked by conflict, distrust, and reduced cooperation among its members.

Negative Emotions and Their Impacts

Susceptibility to anger

- Individual impact: In the present world, being susceptible to anger can lead to increased instances of road rage, impulsive actions, public altercations, and online conflicts. The prevalence of social media and instant communication amplifies the potential for situations to become provocative, leading to impulsive and often regrettable actions.
- Societal impact: The rapid spread of information and inflammatory content can contribute to polarised societies and increased tensions between different groups, impacting social cohesion and trust among individuals.

Lust

- Individual impact: In the digital age, the easy accessibility of explicit content and the proliferation of online dating platforms can exacerbate compulsive sexual behaviours and addiction to pornography. This may lead to broken relationships, unintended pregnancies, particularly among youngsters, and intimacy issues.
- Societal impact: The hypersexualised culture promoted by media and advertising can influence societal attitudes towards objectification and commodification of individuals, potentially increasing instances of sexual harassment, human trafficking, and exploitation.

Jealousy

- Individual impact: Social media platforms can exacerbate feelings of jealousy, as individuals compare their lives to the lives of carefully curated online person as. This can lead to increased anxiety, envy, and a sense of inadequacy.
- Societal impact: Envy and jealousy can fuel a culture of materialism and consumption, leading to increased pressure on individuals to keep up with others and leading to financial strain and debt.

Greed

- Individual impact: In a globalised world, the pursuit of material wealth and success can drive individuals to prioritise personal gain over ethical considerations, potentially leading to financial fraud and unethical business practices.
- Societal impact: The relentless pursuit of profit and economic growth without adequate consideration for social and environmental concerns can contribute to issues such as income inequality, exploitation of resources, and environmental degradation.

Anxiety

- Individual impact: In our fast-paced and uncertain world, individuals may experience heightened anxiety due to factors such as economic instability, job insecurity, and the constant exposure to distressing news through social media.
- Societal impact: High levels of anxiety can impact productivity, healthcare systems, and social interactions, leading to a collective sense of stress and overwhelm within society.

Addressing Negative Emotions

In the present world, technology and globalisation have amplified the impact of negative emotions on individuals and society. The widespread use of social media, digital communication, and instant gratification culture can exacerbate these negative emotions, creating challenges for mental health and social well-being. Addressing these issues requires a multifaceted approach but fundamentally requires the cultivation of constructive thoughts and the elimination of destructive thoughts in individuals. This can be achieved by promoting mental health awareness, responsible media consumption, ethical practices, and a culture of empathy and understanding. Additionally, encouraging emotional intelligence and resilience in individuals can help them navigate the challenges posed by negative emotions.

Exponential Growth Rate

The world at present is full of phenomena that exhibit exponential growth rate. The key characteristic of exponential growth rate is that it accelerates over time, resulting in a rapid increase in the quantity of what is being measured. Compound interest is a classic example of exponential growth rate in the context of finance. The spread of content on social media platforms can demonstrate exponential growth rate as well. Consider a video or meme that goes viral. Initially, it may be shared by a few people, but as more individuals come across it and share it with their networks, the number of views and shares can explode exponentially within a short period of time. This rapid dissemination illustrates the power of exponential growth in the digital age.

The impact of exponential growth rate on our culture and society is significant. The digital age has given rise to an explosion of data and information. With the proliferation of smartphones, social media, and internet-connected devices, massive amounts of data are generated every second. This exponential growth in data has led to the development of big data analytics, machine learning, and artificial intelligence algorithms, enabling organisations to extract valuable insights, improve decision-making, and enhance various industries such as healthcare, finance, and marketing. The global adoption of the internet and the exponential growth in internet usage has revolutionised communication, education, and access to information, bridging gaps and enabling global connectivity and collaboration. The rapid dissemination of knowledge through the internet has led to a more interconnected world, where ideas, cultures, and perspectives can be exchanged instantly. This has influenced our cultural norms, social interactions, and the way we consume and produce media. Exponential growth in global connectivity has fostered increased cultural exchange and globalisation. This has resulted in the blending of cultures, the spread of cultural practices, and the emergence of global trends. It has expanded our understanding and appreciation of diverse cultures, while also making it challenging at times to preserve local traditions and identities.

The rise of e-commerce is a prime example of exponential growth rate in the business world. It has transformed consumer behaviour and market dynamics. With the convenience of online shopping, consumers have shifted from traditional brick-and-mortar retail to e-commerce platforms. The COVID-19 pandemic further accelerated this trend as more people turned to online shopping. The rise of influencer marketing and social media has also shaped consumer preferences and trends, impacting industries such as fashion, beauty, and lifestyle.

Exponential growth in access to educational resources and online learning platforms has transformed the landscape of education. It has expanded opportunities for lifelong learning, enabling individuals to acquire knowledge and skills at their own pace and convenience. This has disrupted traditional educational models and provided access to education for people in remote areas or those with limited resources. However, it also raises challenges related to quality control, credentialing, and ensuring equitable access to educational opportunities.

Exponential growth in communication platforms has facilitated the rise of social movements and activism. Through social media, individuals can mobilise and raise awareness about social, political, and environmental issues. It has empowered marginalised voices, facilitated grassroots organising, and challenged existing power structures. However, it also raises concerns about misinformation, echo chambers, and the potential for online activism to translate into meaningful offline change.

It is important to understand the impact of exponential growth on our culture and society. Many individuals tend to underestimate the amount of food, water, and electricity they waste, often thinking their contribution to overall wastage minimal. However, when you aggregate this behaviour across a large population, the collective impact is unimaginable. Hotels, due to their scale and diverse clientele, generate substantial amounts of food waste daily. When individuals waste food and water regularly, this behaviour contributes to the larger problem of resource depletion. As the population continues to rise, the strain on these resources and ecosystems intensifies. It leads to environmental degradation, scarcity, and higher costs.

The exponential growth of data and information raises concerns about privacy. With the increasing collection and analysis of personal data, individuals' privacy can be compromised. Individuals should have control over their personal information and be aware of how it is being used. Exponential growth can exacerbate existing inequalities. For example, in the realm of technology, the digital divide may widen as certain populations or regions have limited access to the internet and lack digital literacy. Initiatives focused on digital inclusion, affordable internet access, and technological education can help bridge these gaps. Exponential growth in areas such as artificial intelligence and automation raises ethical concerns. It is important to consider the impact of these technologies on employment, human rights, and social dynamics. Developing ethical frameworks and regulations to guide the development and deployment of these technologies can help ensure they are used responsibly and for the benefit of society as a whole. Anticipating and preparing for the potential consequences of rapid growth can help mitigate risks and ensure sustainable development.

Rapid Urbanisation and Self-sufficient Villages

Countries like India are currently experiencing rapid urbanisation, a phenomenon with significant potential benefits but also substantial challenges. While urbanisation can stimulate economic growth and enhance living standards, it requires careful management to avoid the negative consequences seen in other regions. During the rapid urbanisation phases of developed countries, critical missteps had far-reaching consequences. The uncontrolled expansion of cities without adequate planning resulted in sprawling urban areas plagued by insufficient infrastructure and housing. This triggered a host of problems, including crippling traffic congestion, pollution, and sanitation crises. Slums, often disregarded, became breeding grounds for crime and disease. The concentration of wealth and opportunities within cities exacerbated social inequality, perpetuating poverty. Additionally, environmental degradation occurred as green spaces disappeared, historical sites vanished, and marginalised communities were pushed to the city's outskirts. Overreliance on automobiles further exacerbated congestion and pollution. Additionally, urbanisation may lead to encroachment on agricultural land and the loss of traditional practices and cultural heritage as older buildings are replaced by modern structures. These lessons underscore the paramount importance of comprehensive urban planning and sustainability in the ongoing global urbanisation process.

Amidst these challenges, restructuring villages to attain self-sustainability emerges as a crucial solution. Empowered villages can offer a higher standard of living, dissuading migration to overcrowded cities and alleviating pollution. Self-sufficient villages, capable of generating income, can invest in education and healthcare, ultimately improving the quality of life and reducing poverty. Economic and political empowerment of villagers encourages participation in the political process, fostering democratic and just societies. Additionally, self-sufficient villages reduce dependence on external resources, contributing to environmental preservation and conservation. A high standard of living and availability of opportunities in villages will foster stronger social bonds and communities, consequently reducing crime and social unrest. Recognising the pivotal role of women in the rural economy and empowering them can enhance the well-being of everyone within the village.

Safety and Security: The Crime Triangle Theory

A safe and secure environment is undeniably a foundational requirement for the well-being of any society. To grasp the concept of crime, it's crucial to consider the dynamics between victims and perpetrators. In many cases, victims inadvertently provide opportunities for criminals to commit unlawful acts. These opportunities are often analysed using the 'crime triangle' theory, consisting of three elements: the offender, the object, and the opportunity. These elements, collectively referred to as the '3 Os', help us understand what contributes to criminal incidents.

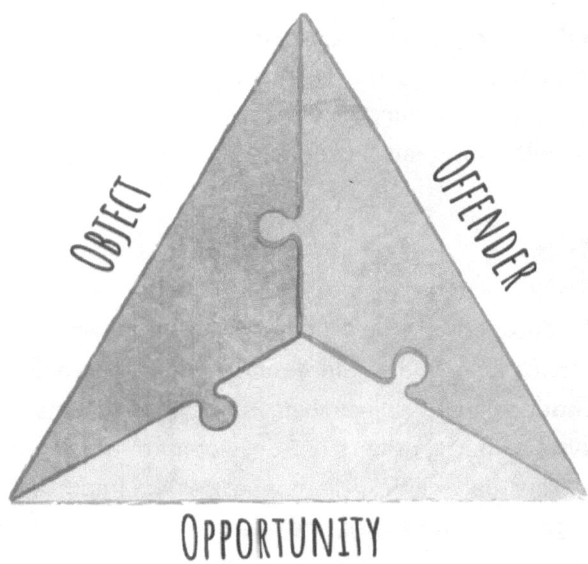

Crimes often stem from vulnerabilities or weaknesses in the environment. These vulnerabilities might include insufficient security measures, inadequate surveillance, poor lighting, or ineffective controls. Criminals may exploit such situations to their advantage, particularly when targeting distracted or vulnerable individuals in places with limited security or when individuals are inattentive to their surroundings.

Some criminals may specifically choose victims they perceive as vulnerable due to factors like age, physical disabilities, or psychological distress, taking advantage of these weaknesses to commit crimes. Distraction, whether caused by electronic devices, walking alone at night, or carrying substantial amounts of cash, can increase a person's vulnerability to criminal activity.

The relationship between victims and perpetrators varies depending on the circumstances. Sharing personal information with strangers, letting them into your home or car, or being under the influence of substances can increase the risk of becoming a crime victim. Criminals often exploit situations in which they see a chance to commit a crime without being caught.

Furthermore, individuals' and groups' routine activities can inadvertently create opportunities for criminal acts. For instance, consistently leaving a house unsecured provides burglars with opportunities. Failing to take precautions that deter criminal behaviour, like leaving valuables visible in a parked car or carrying large amounts of cash in public, also makes individuals susceptible to theft.

Understanding the role of opportunity in the crime triangle theory empowers individuals and communities to take steps towards reducing criminal activity. By focusing on minimising opportunities for crime, it becomes possible to decrease the chances of criminal incidents and enhance overall safety.

Education

In his book *Small is Beautiful*, author E. F. Schumacher emphasises the importance of education that goes beyond mere academic knowledge. He believes that education should address the whole person, nurturing their intellectual, emotional, and spiritual development. Schumacher argues for an education system that considers the development of the entire individual, not just their intellectual abilities. He emphasises the importance of nurturing emotional intelligence, moral values, and a sense of purpose alongside academic knowledge. Schumacher criticises the overemphasis on abstract theories and academic knowledge in education. He advocates a balance between theory and practice, stressing the importance of equipping individuals with practical skills that are relevant to their lives and communities. He also emphasises the importance of understanding local traditions, cultures, and ecological systems, promoting a sense of place and connection. Schumacher argues that education should instil a sense of ethics, social responsibility, and ecological awareness in individuals.

Education plays a pivotal role in the journey of self-discovery and the realisation of one's full potential. Regardless of a student's inclinations or talents, education serves as a guiding light in helping them unearth their capabilities and striving for utmost success.

Education acts as a multifaceted compass for identifying one's potential. Firstly, it serves as a gateway to a diverse array of subjects and domains, unveiling students' passions and interests. Secondly, it imparts vital skills, such as critical thinking and problem-solving, which are indispensable in any career path. Lastly, education is a crucible for talent refinement, both within and beyond the classroom.

By providing a platform to explore a plethora of subjects, education encourages individuals to delve into various disciplines. This exploration fosters self-awareness, revealing strengths, talents, and interests, thus guiding individuals toward their true potential and areas of interest.

Furthermore, education equips individuals with the knowledge and competencies needed to excel in their chosen fields. Whether it's academic acumen, technical expertise, problem-solving prowess, critical thinking, effective communication, or nurturing creativity, education is the forge where these skills are honed. Skill development is instrumental in harnessing one's potential and achieving excellence in their chosen domains.

The scope of education extends beyond the mere acquisition of knowledge; it encompasses personal growth. Education instils qualities such as discipline, perseverance, self-motivation, and a growth-oriented mindset. These attributes are essential to navigating life's challenges, surmounting obstacles, and continually expanding one's potential, leading to success in various dimensions of life.

Education opens doors to a myriad opportunities. It introduces individuals to various career paths, industries, and specialisation areas. Through internships, practical experiences, and industry collaborations, education immerses individuals in real-world scenarios, further refining their potential. This exposure enables them to make informed decisions aligned with their strengths and to seize optimal opportunities.

The concept of lifelong learning proposes that knowledge acquisition doesn't terminate with formal schooling. It encourages individuals to embrace continuous learning and adapt to evolving circumstances. Staying updated and acquiring new knowledge and skills enables individuals to perpetually enhance and expand their potential throughout their lifetimes.

In effective education systems, mentors, teachers, and counsellors play pivotal roles. They guide, nurture, and inspire students, leveraging their wisdom and experience to help students recognise their unique abilities. Personalised attention and guidance are instrumental in assisting students with recognising and maximising their potential.

Teachers

Teachers play a pivotal role in shaping individuals and have a profound impact on their personal and intellectual development. They have the ability to inspire, guide, and instil knowledge, values, and skills in students. Some examples of highly influential teachers include:

- Socrates was an ancient Greek philosopher known for his Socratic method of questioning. His student, Plato, became one of the most influential philosophers in history. Plato's writings, including *The Republic*, reflect the teachings and ideas of his mentor. Socrates' guidance and philosophical discussions with Plato exemplify the transformative power of a teacher–student relationship and the enduring impact it can have on intellectual thought.

- Confucius, an influential Chinese philosopher, educator, and political figure, emphasised the importance of education and ethical conduct. His teachings on morality, social relationships, and personal development have had a lasting impact on Chinese culture and society. Confucius' role as a teacher and mentor to his disciples demonstrates the profound influence teachers can have on shaping values, character, and societal norms.

- Anne Sullivan, a teacher, played a vital role in the life of Helen Keller, who was deaf and blind from a young age. Sullivan identified and encouraged Helen's other senses, like touch and smell, to provide alternate communication for expression and exploration. Sullivan's dedicated mentorship enabled Keller to overcome tremendous obstacles, learn to communicate, and become an influential writer, lecturer, and advocate for people with disabilities.

- Maria Montessori, an Italian educator, developed the Montessori method of education, which emphasises hands-on learning, individualised instruction, and respect for the child's natural development. Her educational philosophy has had a profound influence on early childhood education worldwide.

Lessons for Teachers

- *Innovative teaching methods*. Embrace the opportunities presented by the digital age. Utilise technology, multimedia resources, online platforms, and virtual simulations to create dynamic and engaging lessons. Incorporate interactive learning tools that encourage active participation and collaborative projects, fostering a stimulating learning environment.

- *Inclusivity and diversity.* Recognise the diverse backgrounds, experiences, and abilities of the students. Create an inclusive classroom that values each student's uniqueness. Tailor teaching strategies to accommodate various learning styles, ensuring equal access to educational opportunities for all students.

- *Critical thinking and practical skills.* Encourage critical thinking and analytical skills in students. Design lessons that promote inquiry, creativity, and independent problem-solving. Provide students with opportunities to apply knowledge to real-world situations, allowing them to develop practical skills alongside theoretical understanding.

- *Social and emotional intelligence.* Infuse into your teaching approach activities that promote social and emotional growth. Foster self-awareness, empathy, teamwork, and conflict resolution skills. Cultivate a safe and supportive classroom atmosphere where students feel comfortable expressing their emotions and thoughts, which will contribute to their overall well-being.

- *Continuous professional development.* Embrace lifelong learning by staying up-to-date with the latest research, educational practices, and technological advancements. Attend workshops and conferences and engage with collaborative learning communities to learn about best practices and torefine teaching techniques.

- *Relationship building.* Develop positive relationships with students, parents, and colleagues. Act as a mentor, offering academic and emotional support. Effective communication and collaboration can establish a strong network, benefiting both student growth and holistic well-being.

- *Growth mindset.* Instil a growth mindset in students by demonstrating it yourself. Encourage them to view challenges as opportunities for growth, to learn from failures, and to persist in their efforts. Provide constructive feedback that nurtures this mindset and encourages ongoing improvement.

- *Reflective practice.* Regularly assess teaching methods, lesson outcomes, and student engagement. Adapt approaches based on student feedback and evolving educational research. Continuously refine teaching strategies to cater to changing student needs effectively.

- *Global awareness and ethical responsibility*. Help students understand global issues, cultural diversity, and ethical obligations. Encourage their self-identification as responsible citizens who make positive contributions to their communities and the world.
- *Self-care and well-being*. Prioritise self-care to maintain a healthy work-life balance. Taking out time to recharge and manage stress enhances your ability to support your students effectively. By demonstrating self-care, teachers can underscore its importance to their students, too.

Sports Excellence as a Key Indicator of National Development

Examining a country's development through the lens of sports performances provides a multifaceted perspective that complements conventional metrics like literacy rates and per capita income. Beyond economic and educational benchmarks, excelling in sports serves as a vital indicator of a nation's overall well-being. Active participation in sports contributes significantly to physical health and well-being and is thus reflective of a healthy populace.

This emphasis on sports is most prevalent in countries that have achieved comprehensive development, as it requires infrastructure. For example, nations like the USA and China have demonstrated this by producing a substantial number of world-class athletes. The pursuit of modern sports demands not only athletic prowess but also top-tier infrastructure, prompting investments in urban development and public facilities that benefit entire communities. Engaging the youth in sports not only equips them with indispensable life skills but also galvanises the sports industry itself. Furthermore, sports serve as a potent instrument in international diplomacy, bolstering a nation's global reputation and fostering international cooperation. Accomplished athletes transcend their sport to become inspirational figures, motivating individuals to strive for excellence not only in sports but also in education and various professional pursuits. By integrating sports performance into evaluations of a country's development, we obtain a comprehensive gauge of its overall progress, spanning physical health, social unity, economic prosperity, and cultural heritage. This emphasis on sports not only cultivates a population that is physically resilient but also mentally robust, as athletes require peak levels of fitness and mental fortitude.

Management

The essence of management lies in the art of managing oneself, a concept that has gained significant recognition in recent years, especially within the realm of leadership development. Regrettably, in our personal lives, we often divert our attention outward, neglecting our inner selves, a practice that can be a wellspring of numerous issues.

At its core, this notion underscores that proficient management commences with self-mastery. It underscores that, prior to effectively overseeing and guiding others, we must possess a profound comprehension of our own strengths, weaknesses, and proclivities. It necessitates an acute awareness of our emotions and their potential influence on our decision-making and interactions with others. Furthermore, it demands a well-defined set of personal objectives and priorities, accompanied by the ability to judiciously allocate our time and resources to the realisation of these objectives.

By prioritising self-management, we can emerge as superior leaders and managers, equipped with a heightened ability to recognise and respond to the needs of those we collaborate with. This approach enables us to exemplify the behaviours we aspire to see in others, fostering an environment conducive to positivity and productivity.

Managing the Self

Introspection

Effective introspection involves adopting valuable practices to gain insights into your personality, character, ideas, abilities, strengths, and preferences. By adopting a third-person perspective, you can attain a more objective understanding of yourself, fostering a journey of self-discovery. To create an optimal environment, find a quiet, comfortable space where distractions are minimal, such as a peaceful room or a serene garden. Allocate dedicated, uninterrupted time for self-study on a regular basis, ensuring consistency for a deeper understanding. Begin by reflecting on significant life experiences, both positive and negative, that have shaped your personality and beliefs. Pay attention to your thoughts, emotions, and reactions in various situations to uncover recurring patterns and themes. Assess your strengths and weaknesses, acknowledging areas of expertise as well as opportunities for growth. Delve into your core values and beliefs to grasp their influence on your decisions and actions.

Below is a list of facets you can consider exploring during introspection:

Facet	Themes to Explore
Personality traits	<ul><li>Introverted/extroverted</li><li>Openness to new experiences</li><li>Conscientiousness</li><li>Agreeableness</li><li>Emotional stability</li><li>Dominant/submissive</li><li>Optimistic/pessimistic</li></ul>
Values and beliefs	<ul><li>Personal ethics and moral principles</li><li>Political and social beliefs</li><li>Religious or spiritual beliefs</li><li>Environmental or sustainability perspectives</li><li>Attitudes towards diversity and inclusion</li><li>Cultural background and influences</li><li>Philosophical or existential beliefs</li><li>Views on relationships and family</li><li>Attitudes towards work and success</li></ul>
Interests and hobbies	<ul><li>Activities you enjoy in your free time</li><li>Subjects you like to learn about</li><li>Creative pursuits (e.g. art, music, writing)</li><li>Sports or physical activities you engage in</li></ul>

Facet	Themes to Explore
Strengths and weaknesses	<ul><li>Skills and talents</li><li>Areas where you excel</li><li>Areas where you struggle</li><li>Personal qualities you admire in yourself</li><li>Aspects you would like to improve</li></ul>
Communication and social style	<ul><li>How you interact with others</li><li>Listening skills</li><li>Assertiveness/passiveness</li><li>Ability to empathise and connect with others</li><li>Preferred communication methods (e.g. verbal, written)</li></ul>
Emotional landscape	<ul><li>Emotional intelligence</li><li>Common emotional reactions</li><li>Coping mechanisms and stress management</li><li>Triggers for certain emotions</li><li>Emotional resilience and adaptability</li></ul>
Goals and ambitions	<ul><li>Short-term and long-term goals</li><li>Career aspirations</li><li>Personal growth objectives</li><li>Dreams and desires</li><li>Areas of life you want to improve or develop</li></ul>
Preferences and tastes	<ul><li>Musical, literary, and artistic preferences</li><li>Food and culinary preferences</li><li>Fashion and personal style</li><li>Recreational activities you enjoy</li><li>Environments you are comfortable in</li></ul>
Relationships and social connections	<ul><li>Relationship preferences (e.g., family, friendships, etc)</li><li>Communication and conflict resolution styles (open communication, collaborating, etc)</li><li>Trust and intimacy levels</li><li>Extent of social interactions and social circles(selective socialising, active networking, etc)</li></ul>

While introspection and self-reflection both involve processes aimed at developing self-awareness, they differ in terms of their depth, focus, purpose, and application. Introspection is often deeper and more emotionally centred, while self-reflection is broader and encompasses a wider range of personal experiences and external factors.

Self-review Before Sleep

Self-review before sleep can indeed have a significant impact on the subconscious mind. When you review your day before bed, your subconscious mind is more receptive to new information. This is because your brain is in a relaxed state and more open to suggestions.

This practice allows you to consciously process and make sense of the events that occurred in your day, and it also helps in consolidating memories. Your brain organises and stores information during sleep, particularly during the REM (Rapid Eye Movement) stage. By consciously reviewing your day, you reinforce the neural pathways associated with those memories, making them easier to access in the future. Emotions play a vital role in memory formation and processing. When you review your day, you not only recall events but also examine the emotions you experienced. This process allows you to understand and process your emotions more effectively. By acknowledging and reflecting on your feelings, you can gain insight into any unresolved issues or triggers that may be affecting you subconsciously. Your subconscious mind is highly active during sleep, and it can continue working on unresolved problems or challenges you faced during the day. By reviewing your day before sleep, you provide your subconscious mind with a clear understanding of the issues at hand. This can enhance your problem-solving abilities, as your subconscious mind may continue to work on finding solutions while you sleep. As part of your self-review, you can focus on positive aspects of your day. By consciously recalling and appreciating the positive experiences, accomplishments, or progress you made, you reinforce positive neural pathways in your subconscious mind. This can improve your overall mood, self-confidence, and attitude. Another benefit of self-review before sleep is that it allows you to put in place your intentions for the next day. By reflecting on your day, you can identify areas where you would like to improve or prioritise specific goals. This helps your subconscious mind prepare for the upcoming day, making it more likely that you'll align your actions with your intentions.

Managerial Techniques

Managerial techniques are vital for successful professional management and the effective management of oneself and others. They provide a systematic and structured approach to problem-solving, decision-making, resource optimisation, risk management, effective communication and collaboration, performance evaluation and achieving desired outcomes.

SWOT analysis is a framework used to evaluate an organisation, project, or individual by assessing its internal strengths and weaknesses, as well as external opportunities and threats.

Situational prevention is a managerial technique that focuses on identifying and eliminating potential problems or risks before they occur. It involves proactive measures to create an environment that discourages unwanted behaviours or events.

Both SWOT analysis and situational prevention can be highly beneficial for the present-day generation in various aspects of their lives. SWOT analysis helps with personal development, career planning, entrepreneurship, and academic planning, whereas situational prevention is useful for personal safety, cybersecurity, crime prevention, risk management, and health and well-being as well.

PESTEL analysis is a framework used to assess the external macro-environmental factors that can impact businesses, organisations, or projects. It stands for political, economic, socio-cultural, technological, environmental, and legal factors. This analysis helps identify opportunities and threats arising from these factors.

SMART Goals is a technique for setting specific, measurable, achievable, relevant, and time-bound goals for clarity, focus, and direction.

Stakeholder analysis is a technique used to identify and understand the individuals, groups, or organisations that can significantly influence or be affected by a project, decision, or initiative. It involves mapping stakeholders, assessing their interests, power, and influence, and developing strategies to engage and manage their expectations.

Agile methodology is an iterative project management approach that emphasises flexibility, collaboration, and continuous improvement. It involves breaking down projects into smaller, manageable tasks, working in short iterations or sprints, and regularly reviewing and adapting plans.

The *Triple Bottom Line (TBL) approach* considers the social, environmental, and economic impacts of decisions or initiatives. It evaluates success based on three dimensions: people (social), planet (environmental), and profit (economic). This strategy promotes a holistic and sustainable approach to decision-making, addressing both immediate and long-term impacts. TBL encourages the consideration of ethical and social responsibility aspects, such as social equity, environmental conservation, and fair economic practices.

Root Cause Analysis (RCA) is a problem-solving technique used to identify the underlying causes of issues or failures. It involves systematically investigating the contributing factors and determining the root cause to implement effective corrective actions.

Six Sigma is a data-driven approach used to improve process efficiency and reduce defects or errors. It focuses on minimising variability and achieving high-quality outcomes. While Six Sigma can lead to significant cost savings, improved customer satisfaction, and streamlined processes, it requires dedicated resources, expertise, and cultural buy-in to be implemented effectively.

It's important to note that the specific techniques employed may vary depending on the context, industry, and individual preferences. Individuals should continuously explore and learn new techniques to enhance their managerial skills and adapt to evolving challenges.

AI-Driven Management

Artificial intelligence (AI) has become a pivotal tool in modern managerial techniques, transforming the way organisations make decisions and manage their operations. AI systems can analyse large volumes of data, including online data, such as data from social media and news platforms, quickly and extract valuable insights to predict future events or trends. AI's capabilities are wide-ranging and include data analysis and insights, predictive analytics, resource optimisation, task automation, employee productivity monitoring, risk management, customer relationship management, market research, natural language processing, strategic planning, supply chain optimisation, quality control, performance evaluation, energy management, and healthcare management. These applications empower managers to make data-driven decisions, automate repetitive tasks, enhance customer experiences, optimise resources, and predict future trends. While AI offers immense benefits, it's crucial that managers use it responsibly and ethically, understanding both its potential and limitations. Integrating AI into managerial techniques can lead to increased efficiency, cost savings, and improved competitiveness in today's dynamic business landscape.

Foundational Leadership

'I think most people can learn a lot more than they think they can. They self-limit their ability to learn. One bit of advice: it is important to view knowledge as sort of a semantic tree—make sure you understand the fundamental principles, i.e. the trunk and big branches, before you get into the leaves/details or there is nothing for them to hang on to.'

- Elon Musk

Elon Musk highlighted the importance of understanding fundamental principles, comparing it to the trunk and big branches of a semantic tree of knowledge. This concept can be translated into a valuable managerial process for building strong and effective teams:

Establish a strong foundation (the trunk): Just as a tree needs a robust trunk to support its growth, successful managers should ensure their teams have a strong foundation. This quality of transformational leadership includes understanding the core values, mission, and objectives of the organisation.

- *Prioritising core concepts (the big branches).* 'The Musk Method' urges managers to guide their team members to prioritise core concepts and fundamental skills related to their roles. Before delving into intricate details, ensure your team has mastered the foundational knowledge required to excel in their positions.

- *Continuous learning (cultivate the tree).* Promote a culture of continuous learning. Encourage team members to revisit and strengthen their grasp of fundamental principles regularly. This ongoing education keeps everyone aligned with the organisation's core values and strategies.

- *Problem-solving with principles (root cause analysis).* When challenges arise, guide your teams to address the root causes by applying fundamental principles. This Musk-inspired problem-solving approach leads to more effective solutions and sustainable outcomes.

Survival of the Fittest: Modern Survival Traits

The phrase 'survival of the fittest' was coined by Herbert Spencer, although it is often associated with the theory of natural selection proposed by Charles Darwin. This concept suggests that, in a population of organisms, those individuals with traits that are better suited to their environment are more likely to survive and reproduce, passing on their advantageous traits to their offspring.

In the context of the present generation, the concept of 'survival of the fittest' remains highly pertinent, albeit in a more nuanced and multifaceted manner than its original biological interpretation. It now extends far beyond the realm of natural selection and encompasses a broader spectrum of traits and characteristics that enable individuals to thrive in our complex and rapidly changing environment.

First and foremost, adaptability reigns supreme in this modern era. **Much like organisms needed to adapt to their environments to ensure their survival, individuals today must be highly adaptable.** The ability to quickly learn new skills, embrace emerging technologies, and pivot in response to shifting societal and economic landscapes is paramount. Those who can navigate these transitions with agility are better poised for success.

In an age when information is abundant and easily accessible, possessing strong digital and information literacy skills is a clear advantage. The ability to discern credible sources, critically evaluate information, and leverage technology effectively has become essential. Access to knowledge and the competence to navigate and utilise this information are now key components of the fittest individuals.

Moreover, the entrepreneurial spirit is highly encouraged in today's world. The present generation values those who can identify opportunities, take calculated risks, and innovate in various spheres of life. Whether in business or career pursuits, individuals who exhibit entrepreneurial thinking are more likely to excel and drive positive change.

Building and maintaining meaningful relationships, both in the physical and virtual realms, is a fundamental aspect of survival and success. Networking and strong social skills are assets that open doors to opportunities, foster collaboration, and provide crucial support in the face of challenges.

Mental health and resilience, akin to physical health in previous eras, are of significant importance today. Being able to cope with stress, maintain emotional well-being, and seek help when necessary are crucial to personal development and effective functioning in a fast-paced and often demanding world.

Furthermore, as the world grapples with pressing environmental challenges, individuals who embrace sustainable practices and make eco-conscious choices contribute not only to their personal well-being but also to the health of the planet and future generations.

In our increasingly interconnected global society, understanding global issues, cultural diversity, and international dynamics is an asset. Those who possess a global perspective are better equipped to navigate a world characterised by globalisation, multiculturalism, and rapid information exchange.

Economic and financial literacy are integral to financial stability and growth. Managing finances wisely, making informed investment decisions, and staying informed about economic trends are vital for personal and societal well-being.

Finally, health and wellness, encompassing physical fitness through exercise and a balanced diet, as well as mental wellness practices, are essential. Prioritising one's health contributes not only to longevity but also to a higher quality of life and greater resilience in the face of life's challenges.

It is crucial to approach the concept of 'survival of the fittest' with caution and to avoid misinterpretation. Applying this concept should not justify harmful or unethical behaviours towards others. Instead, it should promote a balance between individual success and collective well-being, empathy, compassion, and fairness.

Being Smart vs Being Intelligent at the Workplace

In the workplace, the success of individuals often depends on their practical abilities and smartness, rather than solely on raw intelligence. Smart individuals excel by applying various techniques effectively. They have a knack for translating their knowledge and skills into real-world solutions, making quick and creative decisions, and navigating the complexities of social dynamics within the workplace. Smartness is marked by adaptability and flexibility, enabling individuals to thrive in fast-paced and ever-changing work environments. Effective communication is another hallmark of smartness, as smart individuals can clearly convey ideas, actively listen, and collaborate seamlessly with colleagues. Furthermore, their high emotional intelligence allows them to manage relationships, resolve conflicts, and foster positive workplace interactions.

Networking skills are also common among smart individuals, who excel at building and maintaining professional relationships and thereby opening doors to valuable opportunities. Additionally, their adeptness at decision-making and problem-solving is a key factor in their workplace success. They weigh options, consider potential outcomes, and make informed choices. Smart individuals are pragmatists, focusing on realistic approaches and finding practical ways to meet objectives while demonstrating resilience and persistence in the face of challenges and setbacks. In essence, it's the practical application of their intelligence, coupled with their adaptability, communication skills, and problem-solving abilities, that often propels smart individuals to excel in the workplace.

Managing Short-term Gratification

Seeking short-lived gratification is common in life. Practices that promote short-term gratification include consuming fast food and entertainment, pursuing certain kinds of non-committal relationships, and engaging in recreational activities. While these pleasures bring instant happiness, excessive indulgence in them can distract us from our responsibilities, harm our health and personal growth, and create dependency, thereby proving detrimental to careers, relationships, and overall well-being.

Learning to control these impulses reduces our reliance on external sources for happiness and builds self-esteem, fosters self-discipline, strengthens decision-making based on long-term thinking, and helps us achieve goals, make responsible choices, and overcome challenges. Practising restraint builds resilience and supports personal growth, which is crucial for dealing with setbacks, managing stress, and pursuing long-term goals.

Key strategies include mindful decision-making, defining long-term goals, and exploring lasting sources of satisfaction like hobbies, relationships, and personal growth. Moderation, not avoidance, is advised in the enjoyment of temporary pleasures.

From a parental perspective, teaching children about temporary pleasures and self-control is vital. Explain the difference between short-lived joy and long-term happiness. Be a role model of self-control and responsible choices. Encourage alternative fulfilling activities and set boundaries on activities providing temporary pleasure. The aim is to help children develop a balanced relationship with such pleasures and cultivate self-control.

Universal Brotherhood and Meta-economics: Harmonising Values and Frameworks

'All are our places, all are our relatives
Neither good nor evil comes from others
Similar are the pains and pleasures
Death is not something new;
And, to live is not to be elated, you know
Or, the sufferings make no difference anyhow
Like rain drops falling onto the ground
Over the stone or plains around
Take their way and form where they fall
Life too goes on and on and that is all
Such are the views of learned ones
So clear in all, what they sense
No need to cajole those who're big name
While not ill-treating incapable'

- Kaniyan Poonkundran (ancient Tamil poet)

From a historical and anthropological perspective, if we trace our ancestry all the way back to its origins, we find common roots and shared forefathers, despite our diverse culture, ethnicities, and geographical locations. This concept is often referred to as the 'most recent common ancestor' (MRCA), indicating the individual from whom all current living humans descended. It's a compelling reminder that, as individuals and societies, we are more interconnected and interrelated than it might appear on the surface.

Universal brotherhood envisions a world where compassion, respect, and solidarity transcend boundaries. Rooted in our shared humanity, it binds us all. Meta-economics, the humanisation of economics, delves into the core assumptions, methodologies, and frameworks of economics, potentially aligning with these values.

Meta-economics intersects with universal brotherhood through an examination of ethical foundations. By evaluating economic theories against principles like equity, justice, and human dignity, it aids in developing economic frameworks in line with universal brotherhood.

In today's globalised world, meta-economics scrutinises the impacts of globalisation, trade policies, and financial systems on disparities and power dynamics. Identifying factors that hinder or promote universal brotherhood, it helps shape economic systems fostering cooperation and fairness across borders.

Achieving a delicate equilibrium between available natural resources, their resilience, and human development is a pressing challenge that demands thoughtful consideration. Meta-economics explores alternative metrics of well-being, going beyond traditional economic indicators. Acknowledging that material wealth alone cannot encompass human needs, it incorporates dimensions like health, education, social cohesion, and environmental sustainability. It emphasises the importance of sustainable resource management, focusing on preserving resources for future generations rather than short term gains.

In our interconnected era, meta-economics gains relevance by integrating insights from sociology, psychology, and anthropology. These perspectives offer invaluable insights into human behaviour, societal norms, and cultural dynamics, contributing to understanding and nurturing universal brotherhood.

Lastly, meta-economics prompts economists and policymakers to reflect on their values, biases, and assumptions. This introspective approach fosters self-awareness and critical thinking, encouraging the consideration of policy approaches prioritising cooperation, inclusivity, and mutual respect.

Managing Money Wisely

Effective management of financial resources, especially money, is essential to attaining financial stability and building wealth over time. This journey demands discipline and patience, and many individuals encounter challenges in managing their money wisely. Limited financial literacy can hinder their grasp of fundamental financial concepts. Impulsive spending and unplanned purchases can lead to overspending and financial instability. Living beyond one's means can result in the accumulation of debt and financial stress, especially with high interest rates. Failing to establish an emergency fund can leave people exposed to unexpected expenses and financial crises.

Societal pressures and peer influence may lead to financial choices misaligned with long-term goals. Falling victim to financial scams can result in significant losses.

To address these issues, individuals should prioritise improving financial literacy, creating a budget, managing debt responsibly, establishing an emergency fund, and setting clear financial goals. Additionally, it is crucial to understand the psychology of money by delving into the emotional, cognitive, and behavioural aspects of money management and decision-making, because these aspects significantly influence financial behaviours, attitudes toward money, and overall financial well-being.

People's emotional responses to money can vary due to past experiences, cultural backgrounds, and personal beliefs. Cognitive biases, like loss aversion and overconfidence, can lead to irrational financial decisions. Some individuals adopt a scarcity mindset, leading to excessive frugality or reluctance to invest in essential areas.

Comparing one's wealth to that of others can lead to lifestyle inflation. Recognising and addressing negative beliefs about money is crucial. The ability to prioritise long-term goals over short-term impulses is essential to wealth-building.

Some individuals avoid dealing with financial matters altogether, while others become overly obsessed with money, leading to imbalanced priorities and stress.

Today's youth can seek financial education through books, online resources, workshops, or courses. Understanding basic financial concepts will empower them to make informed choices. Learning about early investing and compound interest and having an emergency fund are beneficial. An awareness of economic developments should be cultivated to inform financial decisions, and financial goals and plans should be reviewed as circumstances change. Self-reflection will help identify limiting beliefs and biases.

Set clear financial goals, track expenses, be mindful of peer influence, practise delayed gratification, addressing money-related anxiety pro actively, and view mistakes as learning opportunities. By understanding the psychology of wealth, you can make sound financial choices, reduce money-related stress, and work towards your financial aspirations.

Managing the Influence of Culture on Lifestyle

As discussed earlier, culture exerts a profound influence on how one manages one's lifestyle, shaping values, beliefs, traditions, and actions. It moulds the very fabric of daily routines, impacting choices related to health, habits, and overall well-being and governing waking and sleeping patterns, work schedules, and leisure pursuits.

Effectively managing the influence of culture on one's lifestyle begins with understanding one's cultural background and how it shapes beliefs and behaviours around dieting, exercise, stress management, and overall well-being. Embracing cultural diversity entails being open to learning about various cultures and their lifestyle practices, allowing individuals to adopt beneficial elements while respecting their own heritage. Evaluating lifestyle choices objectively by considering evidence-based benefits and potential drawbacks ensures that one's decisions align with one's health needs. Defining personal values and priorities independently of cultural influences allows one to integrate those aspects of one's culture that resonate with one's values. Incorporating health-promoting customs from one's culture, such as family meals or social connections, can enhance overall well-being. Adapting cultural practices to suit modern living while preserving traditions when possible is key, and connecting with like-minded communities, regardless of cultural backgrounds, provides crucial support in maintaining a healthy lifestyle.

In essence, recognising the influence of culture on lifestyle management and proactively navigating these influences empowers individuals to make informed choices that align with their well-being and personal values.

Lessons from Once-flourishing Civilisations

The destruction of once-flourishing civilisations throughout history offers several important lessons for present generations.

- Societies that become deeply divided or plagued by inequality often face internal conflicts and weakened institutions. The fall of the Roman Empire serves as an example of increasing disparities between the rich and poor, corruption, and a lack of social cohesion contributing to civilisational decline. To prevent a similar fate, the present generation should strive for inclusive societies that promote equality, fairness, and social justice.

- Many civilisations collapsed due to environmental degradation and resource depletion. The ancient Maya civilisation, for instance, experienced a decline in agricultural productivity as a result of deforestation and soil erosion. The present generation should prioritise sustainable practices, such as responsible resource management, conservation, and reduction of carbon emissions, to prevent environmental catastrophe.

- The preservation and celebration of cultural heritage are crucial for the continuity of civilisations. The destruction of the Library of Alexandria in ancient Egypt resulted in the loss of countless texts and knowledge. The present generation should value and protect cultural artifacts, historical records, and diverse traditions to ensure the preservation of human history and the promotion of cultural understanding.

- Civilisations that fail to adapt to changing circumstances and technological advancements often face decline. The Viking civilisation, for example, relied heavily on raiding and trading but was unable to adapt to the changing economic and political landscape. To avoid stagnation, the present generation should embrace innovation and technological progress and remain open to new ideas and ways of thinking.

- Civilisations depend for stability and longevity on strong governance and competent leadership. The downfall of the Byzantine Empire can be attributed, in part, to a series of weak emperors, political infighting, and a lack of strategic vision. The present generation should prioritise effective governance structures, transparency, accountability, and capable leadership to ensure the well-being and sustainability of societies. Technological advancements can bring about great progress but also have the potential to create vulnerabilities. For instance, the collapse of the Bronze Age civilisations in the Eastern Mediterranean is believed to be partly due to disruptions caused by the Sea Peoples, who had superior maritime technology. It is crucial that the present generation recognise the potential risks associated with technology and ensure responsible development and usage.

- Economic mismanagement played a significant role in the downfall of civilisations like the Byzantine Empire and the Inca Empire. Issues such as overreliance on a single resource or unsustainable economic practices led to their collapse. The present generation should prioritise economic sustainability, diversify their economies, promote responsible financial practices, and ensure equitable distribution of resources.

Contemporary Culture: Wealth and Frugality

In some cultural contexts, the accumulation of wealth and material possessions is highly valued and seen as a symbol of success and social standing. In such cultures, the pursuit of wealth becomes intertwined with notions of happiness, status, and personal fulfilment. It is fuelled by societal narratives that equate material abundance with personal achievement and worth. Consequently, individuals may perceive the acquisition of wealth as a necessity, believing that it will bring them security, happiness, and societal recognition.

I know that the most joy in my life has come to me from my violin.

- Albert Einstein

On the other hand, there are cultures that prioritise alternative values beyond material wealth. These cultures emphasise community, spiritual well-being, relationships, and experiences as key sources of fulfilment. In these cultural contexts, the pursuit of wealth may be viewed as secondary to personal growth, social harmony, and the development of one's inner qualities.

In cultures that place greater emphasis on non-material aspects of life, individuals may derive meaning and happiness from their connections with others, the pursuit of knowledge, artistic expression, or contributions to the common good. They may prioritise experiences, personal growth, and the cultivation of virtues such as compassion, wisdom, and integrity over the accumulation of material possessions.

In many contemporary cultures, there is a pervasive influence of consumerism and materialism. These cultural norms often accord a high value to wealth, financial success, and material possessions. In societies driven by capitalism and market economies, the pursuit of wealth is often seen as a primary goal and a measure of personal achievement and social status.

The prevalence of media, advertising, and social media platforms further reinforces the idea that material possessions and financial abundance are necessary for happiness and fulfilment. These cultural messages shape our desires and aspirations, creating an aura of necessity around wealth and money. Individuals may feel pressure to acquire material goods, maintain a certain standard of living, or accumulate wealth as a means of achieving social validation and personal happiness.

Furthermore, as the costs of housing, education, healthcare, and basic amenities escalate, individuals may feel compelled to pursue higher incomes and accumulate wealth to meet their essential needs and provide for their families.

However, there are emerging cultural movements and countercultural trends that challenge the dominance of consumerism and advocate alternative approaches to well-being and success. These movements encourage sustainable living, minimalism, and a focus on experiences rather than material possessions, reshaping the perception of wealth.

A frugal lifestyle is characterised by living within one's means, being mindful of expenses, and making deliberate choices to save money.

Warren Buffett, nicknamed the 'Oracle of Omaha', whose success as an investors has made him one of the wealthiest individuals in the world, is often cited as a role model for those interested in long-term, value-focused investing. He is also known for his disciplined approach to spending and his relatively modest lifestyle. Some people even playfully refer to him as the 'Frugal King' because of his frugality.

Ancient vs. Modern Culture

Interconnectedness

Ancient cultures often exhibited a deep respect and reverence for the vital resources that sustained their existence. These cultures recognised the interconnectedness of humans with nature and developed various practices and beliefs to honour and preserve these resources.

Many ancient cultures relied heavily on agriculture for their sustenance. They understood the importance of fertile land, water, and sunlight for successful crop cultivation. As a result, they developed agricultural practices and rituals to ensure abundant harvests. Harvest festivals were celebrated to express gratitude to the land and the deities associated with fertility and agriculture. Water was considered a sacred and life-giving element in many ancient cultures. Rivers, springs, and wells were often worshipped as deities or regarded as spiritual entities. Water was used in purification rituals, and people showed great respect for its sources, ensuring their cleanliness and protection. The sun, as the ultimate source of heat and light energy, held great significance in ancient cultures. Sun deities were often worshipped, and solar calendars played a crucial role in agricultural cycles. Many cultures aligned their architectural structures and rituals with the movements of the sun. Animistic beliefs were common in ancient cultures, which associated natural elements such as trees, mountains, rivers, and animals with spirits or divine essences and performed various rituals and made offerings of food, flowers, and other symbolic items to deities associated with agriculture, water, and the sun to appease and honour the forces of nature. These ancient cultures often practised sustainable resource management through rotational farming, crop diversification, and water conservation techniques. They recognised the importance of preserving the land's fertility and maintaining a balance between resource consumption and regeneration.

Modern societies, especially in urban areas, have become increasingly disconnected from nature and the processes that sustain life. With the rise of technology and urbanisation, people are now more focused on convenience and immediate gratification, leading to a diminished appreciation for the natural resources that support their existence.

The current generation tends to take these resources for granted due to their relative abundance and ease of access. This can lead to overconsumption, wasteful practices, and an unsustainable lifestyle. Many people fail to recognise the limited nature of these resources and the long-term consequences of their actions on the environment.

Insufficient education about the importance of these resources and their interdependence is a likely contributor to the lack of awareness among the present generation. Modern society is characterised by a focus on short-term gains and immediate gratification. This mindset can hinder long-term planning and sustainable practices. Failure to understand the consequences of environmental degradation can perpetuate destructive practices and the cycle of resource exploitation.

Hence, it is necessary to learn from ancient cultures:

- Promote environmental education at all levels, from schools to community programmes.
- Emphasise the interconnectedness of humans and nature, the finite nature of resources, and the consequences of unsustainable practices.
- Encourage individuals to spend time in nature, whether through outdoor activities, gardening, or participation in conservation efforts.
- Promote sustainable practices in daily life, such as reducing waste, conserving water and energy, supporting local and organic food production, and adopting renewable energy sources.
- Explore and study indigenous and traditional practices that prioritise the preservation of resources, such as agroecology, water conservation techniques, and traditional medicine, and incorporate these practices into contemporary solutions. While not all ancient rituals may be applicable or feasible in modern society, adopting some of them can help foster a sense of connection with nature and respect for vital resources. These could include rituals to express gratitude to nature for its bounty, ceremonies celebrating the changing seasons, or communal activities focused on environmental conservation.
- Promote dialogue and knowledge-sharing between different cultures and generations.
- Promote conscious consumption by encouraging individuals to consider the environmental and social impact of their choicesand opt for reusable and environmentally friendly alternatives.
- Support companies and products that prioritise sustainability and ethical practices.

Diversity and Universality in Spirituality

It's noteworthy that many individuals may hold narrow views of spirituality, often associating it solely with religious customs or specific doctrines. However, spirituality is an intricate and multifaceted concept that extends far beyond religious boundaries. It is essential to appreciate and honour the diversity of spiritual beliefs and practices, which can encompass religious, philosophical, nature-inspired, and even secular approaches.

At its essence, spirituality involves a personal journey of exploration into the realms of meaning, purpose, and connection that transcend the material world. This quest for spirituality can manifest in various ways, with individuals finding spiritual fulfilment through practices such as meditation, mindfulness, introspection, or their connection to nature.

While religious perspectives play a significant role in shaping the experience of spirituality for many, it's crucial to acknowledge that not all who identify as spiritual adhere to any particular religious faith or dogma. Some may discover their spiritual connection through profound moments of awe and wonder inspired by the natural world while others may seek inner peace and self-discovery through mindfulness techniques.

Furthermore, it's important to recognise that limiting beliefs about age and gender can also influence perceptions of one's spiritual journey. Society's preconceived notions about who can engage in or benefit from spiritual practices can be restrictive. In truth, spirituality is a universal endeavour that transcends age and gender, and individuals of all backgrounds and stages of life can embark on this meaningful exploration. Itis a deeply personal odyssey, and each person's path is uniquely their own.

Yearly Review of Top 10 Skills

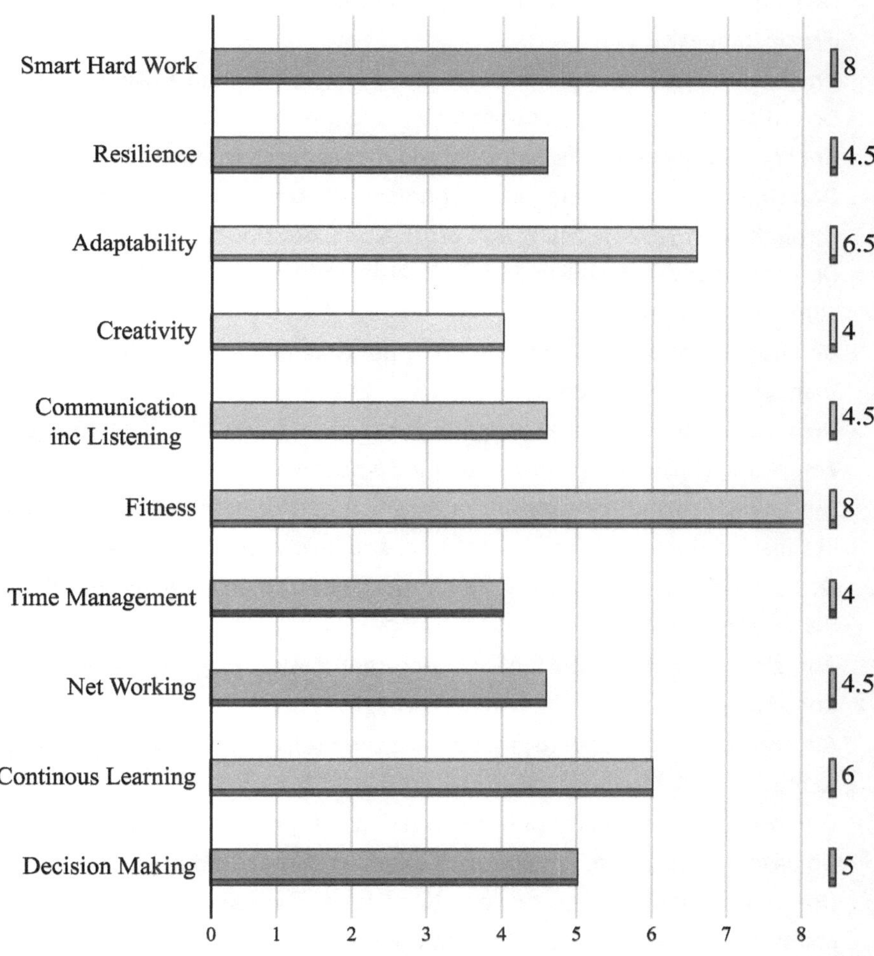

Checklist for Management

Self-awareness

- Do I strongly believe that every problem has a solution?
- Do I have a clear understanding of my professional strengths and limitations?
- Do I regularly review and adjust my goals based on my progress and changing circumstances?
- Am I aware that peace of mind is the only way to maintain a winning streak?
- Do I maintain a healthy work-life balance to prevent burnout?
- Am I constantly practising self-care and managing stress levels?
- Do I stay updated on emerging technologies and trends relevant to my field through continuous learning and professional development?
- Do I utilise techniques like SWOT analysis and the one-minute principle to complete tasks effectively?
- Do I use the Pomodoro technique or other time management techniques to manage my time efficiently?
- Do I cultivate my mental toughness by staying committed to my goals, embracing challenges head-on, keeping a positive mindset, etc?
- Am I aware of the mind games with which people manipulate each other, like playing the victim card, gaslighting, and involving third parties?
- Do I prioritise tasks based on their importance and urgency, using tools like the Eisenhower Matrix?
- Am I also aware that important but non-urgent tasks should not be neglected?
Communication
- Am I an active listener who gives people their full attention when they speak to me?
- Do I express myself clearly and effectively, ensuring my message is understood?
- Do I avoid impatience, argumentativeness, and interruption?
- Do I use visual aids or presentations when necessary to enhance the comprehensibility of what I am communicating?

Conflict Resolution

- Am I skilled at resolving conflicts within my team in a fair and constructive manner?
- Do I admit when I don't know something?
- Do I actively work to prevent and address conflicts before they escalate?
- Do I avoid engaging in arguments or dismissive behaviour when conflicts arise?

Delegation

- Am I proficient at assigning tasks and responsibilities based on team members' strengths and capabilities?
- Do I trust my team members to carry out their assigned tasks without micromanagement by me?
- Do I avoid being impatient or overly controlling when delegating tasks?

Adaptability

- Am I open to change and able to adapt to new circumstances or challenges?
- Do I encourage a culture of flexibility and innovation within my team?

Feedback and Recognition

- Am I proactive in providing constructive feedback and recognition to team members?
- Do I ensure that feedback is specific, timely, and focused on behaviours or outcomes?

Learning and Development

- Am I committed to my own professional development and to learning new skills?
- Do I encourage and support the growth and development of my team members?

Ethical Leadership

- Am I transparent and honest in my communications with team members and stakeholders?
- Do I lead by example in demonstrating integrity, trustworthiness, and accountability?
- Do I influence others by using my skills of persuasion instead of resorting to the exercise of authority?

Crisis Management

- Do I empower myself by acknowledging my emotions when I face unprecedented challenges as a leader?
- Am I prepared to lead and make decisions during times of crisis?
- Do I have a contingency plan in place to ensure the safety and well-being of my team members?
- Am I able to remain calm and make rational decisions under pressure?

Goal Alignment

- Are the goals and objectives I set for myself and my team aligned with the overall mission and vision of the organisation?
- Do I communicate to my team members the strategic direction of the organisation and how each member's work contributes to it?

Continuous Improvement

- Am I regularly evaluating and improving my own management skills and practices?
- Do I encourage a culture of continuous improvement within my team?
- Am I open to experimenting with new techniques and approaches to enhance team performance?

Resource Management

- Do I prioritise reducing the consumption of resources whenever possible by using technology?
- Am I sorting and recycling materials properly to minimise landfill waste?
- Am I mindful of energy conservation techniques like the use of energy-efficient appliances, paperless practices, sustainable transportation methods, etc?

Checklist for Creating Wealth/Financial Resources

General

- Am I aware that all saving and spending should be done with an understanding of how these habits impact my future financial health?
- Am I actively taking steps to secure my financial stability instead of harbouring envy for those who have more wealth?
- Do I recognise that monetary success isn't solely reliant on hard work, but also on factors like working in the right role, saving, and effective financial planning?
- Am I prioritising my financial well-being and acknowledging its significance?
- Do I understand the potential harm in either maintaining or severing relationships solely based on financial considerations?
- Am I aware of the role money plays in propping up my self-esteem and happiness?

- Do I make financial decisions that are in line with my comfort level?
- Do I extend my simplicity to my daily routines (e.g. by using public transport to commute to my office instead of using my car every day)?
- Am I aware that it is important to prioritise spending on high-quality basic necessities without hesitation(e.g. pillows, bed, shoes, etc)?

Avoiding Impulse Purchases

- Do I think carefully before making non-essential purchases?
- Do I avoid unnecessary expenses that don't add any value to my life?
- Am I able to delay gratification to prioritise long-term financial goals?

Awareness of Societal Pressures

- Am I conscious of how peer influences and societal pressures affect my spending habits?
- Do I make financial decisions based on my needs and values rather than external influences?

Tracking Spending Habits

- Do I regularly track my expenses to understand where my money goes?
- Am I aware of areas where I can cut back on unnecessary spending?

Emergency Fund

- Do I have an emergency fund set aside for unexpected expenses?
- Is my emergency fund sufficient to cover three to six months of living expenses?

Savings Plan

- Do I have a structured savings plan to help me achieve my short-term and long-term financial goals?
- Am I consistently contributing to my savings and investment accounts?

Reviewing Financial Goals

- Do I review my financial goals periodically to ensure they align with my changing circumstances?
- Have I set myself specific, measurable, achievable, relevant, and time-bound (SMART) goals?

Awareness of Economic Impact

- Do I keep myself informed about economic trends and developments?
- Am I aware of how these developments can impact my investments and financial decisions?

Understanding the Power of Compound Interest

- Do I understand how compound interest can work for or against me in savings and debt?
- Am I taking advantage of compound interest to grow my investments?

Money-Related Anxiety or Stress

- Do I experience anxiety or stress related to money matters?
- Have I sought professional help or adopted coping strategies to manage financial stress?

Identifying Limiting Beliefs and Biases

- Am I aware of any limiting beliefs or biases that might affect my financial decisions?
- Am I actively working to challenge and overcome these beliefs?

Awareness of Financial Scams and Fraud

- Do I stay informed about common financial scams and fraud?
- Do I take the necessary precautions to protect my financial information and assets?

Strong Passwords for E-Wallet and Accounts

- Do I use strong, unique passwords for my electronic wallets and financial accounts?
- Do I utilise multi-factor authentication for added security?

Understanding Lifestyle Inflation

- Am I conscious of lifestyle inflation and its potential impact on my financial goals?
- Do I avoid unnecessary increases in expenses as my income rises?

Diversification of Investments

- Do I diversify my investment portfolio to manage risk and maximise returns?
- Am I regularly rebalancing my investments to maintain the desired asset allocation?

Financial Education and Learning

- Do I invest time in learning about personal finance and wealth-building strategies?
- Am I open to seeking advice from financial professionals when needed?

Chapter
06

The Conclusion: Holistic Individuals

Leonardo da Vinci is often cited as an example of a holistic individual, a Renaissance man who excelled in multiple areas of expertise, including art, science, engineering, and philosophy, physical fitness, etc. da Vinci's approach to learning and knowledge was rooted in a deep curiosity and a desire to understand the interconnectedness of the world around him. He believed that, to truly understand one aspect of the world, one had to understand its relationships with other aspects.

In addition to his artistic pursuits, da Vinci was also a prolific inventor and engineer, designing a range of machines and devices, including flying machines, weapons, and water pumps. His inventions were often inspired by his observations of nature and the human body, and he sought to create machines that mimicked the natural world.

He believed in the importance of compassion and empathy for all living creatures and saw humanity as an integral part of the natural world rather than separate from it.

Da Vinci's holistic approach to knowledge and understanding has inspired many individuals to follow in his footsteps and pursue interdisciplinary study and exploration. His legacy continues to be celebrated today as an example of the power of curiosity, creativity, and a willingness to approach problems from multiple perspectives.

Foundations of Holistic Living

- *Embrace transformation.* Holistic individuals understand that growth is a perpetual journey. They eagerly welcome change, recognising it as the very essence of life's beauty.
- *Nurture connections.* Deep interconnectedness is the cornerstone of holistic living. Holistic individuals foster meaningful relationships, knowing their actions reverberate through the tapestry of existence, fostering unity and harmony.

- *Adapt with grace.* Like skilled navigators, holistic individuals gracefully adjust to life's turns. Resilience is their virtue; they evolve in harmony with their surroundings and the challenges they bring.
- *Maintain balance.* Within themselves, they find the wellspring of equilibrium. Holistic individuals cultivate harmony in body, mind, and emotion, nurturing a life of vibrancy and equilibrium.
- *Harness energy.* They tap into the well of energy flowing around and within them. This energy fuels their passions, infusing purpose and vitality into every endeavour.
- *Maintain inner harmony.* Cultivating inner peace is an art. Holistic individuals weave together practices that promote their well-being, creating a serene sanctuary amidst life's hustle and bustle.
- *Cherish creation.* The act of creation is sacred to them. Nurturing relationships, they celebrate the gift of life, leaving behind wisdom and love for future generations to embrace.
- *Savour sensations.* Attuned to the world, they savour each moment. Holistic individuals relish life's sensory pleasures, responding to nature's whispers with gratitude and mindfulness.
- *Celebrate complexity.* The intricacies of their nature are treasured. They embrace complexity as a canvas for boundless potential, growth, and learning.
- *Evolve consciously.* Embarking on an evolutionary journey, they delve into self-discovery. Holistic individuals embrace growth, refining their essence as they evolve into authenticity.
- *Cultivate awareness.* A heightened awareness is their pursuit. Nurturing conscious thought, holistic individuals strengthen their connection to the universe's profound wonders.
- *Embrace renewal.* With grace, they embrace life's cycles. Holistic individuals honour natural rhythms, gracefully releasing the old to welcome the new in an eternal dance.
- *Champion diversity.* Celebrating humanity's vibrant tapestry is their ethos. Holistic individuals honour diversity, recognising that each person as a unique stroke in life's masterpiece.
- *Harmony with rhythms.* Attuned to nature's cadence, they sway to its melodies. From dawn to dusk, birth to transition, holistic individuals synchronise themselves with life's cycles, living harmoniously with the cosmos.

In embodying these essential requirements, holistic individuals become stewards of their own well-being and the world around them. Their journey unfolds as a harmonious symphony, with each note contributing to the greater melody of existence.

The Holistic Self-Reflection Odyssey

Holistic individuals engage in a continuous process of introspection that involves deep examination of their thoughts, emotions, experiences, and actions. This inward exploration goes beyond surface-level contemplation, cultivating profound self-awareness, personal growth, and enhanced emotional intelligence. By posing thought-provoking questions, challenging preconceptions, and dissecting behaviours, holistic individuals uncover the underlying motives and patterns that shape their lives.

Central to this process is mindfulness—an active presence and non-judgmental stance while scrutinising thoughts and feelings. Through mindful observation, holistic individuals attain a greater comprehension of themselves without succumbing to self-critique. They develop emotional awareness, delving into the intricacies of their feelings and how these emotions influence their thoughts and behaviours. This heightened emotional intelligence empowers them to manage their emotions more effectively and respond to situations with heightened consciousness.

Learning from experiences, whether successes or setbacks, is a crucial facet of holistic self-reflection. Extracting invaluable lessons from their past endeavours, these individuals cultivate personal growth. They keenly identify areas of improvement and take time to celebrate their accomplishments, fostering a continual journey of growth and self-evolution.

In the pursuit of self-awareness, holistic individuals adeptly pinpoint their strengths, using these attributes as building blocks for personal advancement. Simultaneously, they acknowledge their limitations, seeking ways to address these areas or integrate compensatory strategies. This balanced view of themselves forms the foundation for their holistic approach to life.

Holistic self-reflection serves as a compass for setting goals that are in alignment with the innermost values and aspirations of individuals. This clarity propels them towards a more fulfilling existence in which their actions are guided by what truly resonates with their essence. Empowered by this understanding, they forge connections with others, fortified by empathy and an acute perception of the emotions and perspectives of those around them.

These individuals also extend their introspective gaze to their relationships, utilising self-reflection to uncover biases, communication patterns, and triggers. By fostering understanding within themselves, they create nurturing spaces for authentic connections with others, cultivating relationships founded on mutual respect and empathy.

Regular self-reflection, a form of self-care, provides holistic individuals with a sanctuary in which they can release stress, recalibrate their perspective, and achieve emotional equilibrium. Through journalling, mindfulness meditation, seeking feedback, and carving out dedicated time, they infuse their lives with intentionality and authenticity.

Holistic individuals recognise that self-reflection is not a one-time effort but a perpetual journey of personal development and emotional intelligence. This journey guides their interactions with the world.

Embracing Cultural, Religious, and Societal Influences: Harmonious Coexistence

Throughout the annals of history, the human inclination to form groups and tribes based on shared characteristics like culture, religion, language, or ethnicity has shaped our identities and sense of belonging. However, these affiliations can inadvertently lead to an 'us vs. them' mentality, whereby outsiders are perceived as different or threatening.

While human nature plays a role in conflicts, we must acknowledge the multitude of factors at play—from historical grievances and power struggles to socioeconomic disparities and territorial disputes. Sometimes, conflicts and discrimination arise due to groups with vested interests seeking to further their agendas.

To achieve emotional health, we must introspect to understand how cultural, societal, and religious influences have shaped our beliefs and behaviours. This introspection calls for critical thinking and self-awareness and the recognition that these influences can have both positive and negative impacts.

Embracing open-mindedness is vital, as it enables us to consider diverse perspectives before forming conclusions. It is equally crucial to evaluate the sources of information we consume and avoid the confines of echo chambers.

Acknowledging the powerful sense of group identity these affiliations foster, we should strive to rise above blind tribalism and treat others with respect and empathy. Balancing respect for positive traditions with opposition to harmful practices promotes personal growth.

Emotionally healthy individuals resist succumbing to peer pressure from cultural or religious communities, prioritising authenticity. Seeking evidence, reason, and critical thought enables us to form beliefs that align with our values rather than adopt inherited ones.

In our pursuit of a just and harmonious society, we must challenge discriminatory practices and ideologies that perpetuate division. By promoting inclusivity and understanding among different cultural and religious groups, we can bridge gaps and foster peaceful coexistence.

By being cautious and aware, we navigate the complexities of cultural, societal, and religious influences while maintaining emotional and intellectual integrity. Embracing empathy, self-awareness, and critical thinking, we pave the path towards a more compassionate and harmonious world.

The Fusion of Time Management and Mind Management

The qualities that lie at the intersection of time management and mind management resonate with the attributes of holistic individuals:

- *Prioritisation.* Holistic individuals possess the acumen to evaluate tasks through the lens of urgency and significance. Their cognitive faculties aid in distinguishing tasks requiring immediate attention from those that can be delegated or deferred, thereby optimising their effectiveness.
- *Focus.* The art of maintaining focus is a hallmark of holistic individuals. They adeptly manage cognitive resources to shield against distractions, channelling their mental energy towards tasks at hand and safeguarding against tangential diversions that can dilute productivity.

- *Planning.* Holistic individuals demonstrate strategic planning, which serves as a cornerstone of their approach to time management. By projecting potential obstacles, allocating time prudently, and constructing rational timetables, they excel in task completion within stipulated time frames.
- *Discipline.* Cultivating discipline and self-control is integral to the holistic approach to time management. Such individuals adeptly navigate cognitive processes to thwart procrastination, control impulses, and uphold commitment to goals, fostering sustained motivation and concentration.
- *Decision-making.* Holistic individuals excel in judiciously allocating limited time among diverse tasks. Their cognitive faculties are engaged in evaluating options, analysing potential outcomes, and selecting optimal courses of action. Sound decision-making is both a pillar of time management and an attribute of effective mind management.
- *Stress reduction.* Mind management techniques are pivotal in alleviating stress stemming from time constraints. Employing mindfulness, positive self-talk, and relaxation strategies, holistic individuals regulate their mental state, mitigating anxiety and enabling clearer decision-making and efficient work.
- *Adaptability.* Holistic individuals exhibit mental flexibility, crucial for responsive time management. In the face of unexpected events, their cognitive agility allows swift adjustments of priorities and schedules. This synergy between mental adaptability and time management is central to their approach.
- *Goal alignment.* Pursuing objectives with focus characterises holistic individuals. They adeptly set clear goals, understand motivations, and align tasks with their aspirations. This alignment optimises their use of time and effort, facilitating maximum impact.
- *Optimal use of technology.* Holistic individuals recognise the value of utilising technology to enhance their time and mind management. They leverage tools and applications that aid in task organisation, efficiency, and communication. By integrating suitable technologies into their approach, they streamline processes and stay in sync with their goals and responsibilities.

By embracing decision-making, stress reduction techniques, adaptability, goal alignment, and optimal technology utilisation, we can amplify our effectiveness in managing both our thoughts and our time.

Soaring Resilience: Airplane Tires and Holistic Individuals

Holistic individuals are characterised by their resilience. Like sturdy airplane tires that handle heavy loads during take-off and landing, these incredible individuals effortlessly carrying the weight of responsibilities on their shoulders. And just as the specialised materials in airplane tires ensure optimal performance, holistic individuals possess a unique blend of physical, mental, and emotional qualities that make them invincible in the face of life's challenges. Their healthy habits, self-care routines, and a support system are akin to quality control measures for airplane tires. With these qualities and practices, holistic individuals emerge from each challenge with renewed strength and wisdom, ready to face whatever comes their way.

Mastering the Art of Cherishing Every Moment

Time is a fascinating aspect of human experience. When we spend time with our loved ones or engage in activities we are passionate about, our sense of time seems to alter. The reason for this lies in the concept of 'flow', or being in a state of complete immersion in an activity. This heightened level of presence and emotional connection makes time seem to fly by because we are not constantly checking the clock or thinking about other things.

On the other hand, when we are unhappy or bored, time tends to drag on because our minds may wander, and we become more aware of the passing minutes. This is why it is said that 'time flies when you're having fun' or 'a watched pot never boils.'

Passion and enthusiasm for our jobs can also have a similar effect. When we are deeply engaged and fulfilled by our work, we are less conscious of time passing and our focus remains on the task at hand.

Overall, our perception of time is intricately connected to our emotions, level of engagement, and contentment with the present moment. When we find joy and fulfilment in our experiences, time seems to speed up, and we are left with beautiful memories that felt like they lasted mere seconds. This is how it feels to live in the present and cherish meaningful connections in our lives.

Living in a manner whereby time seems to transcend its usual boundaries and every moment becomes a treasured gift is an art we can master through:

- *Mindfulness.* Mindfulness stands at the forefront, encouraging us to immerse ourselves fully in the present, shedding distractions and savouring the joy of the people and activities surrounding us.

- *Passion.* Passion becomes our compass, urging us to explore and embrace activities that ignite our hearts, infusing each passing second with fulfilment and reward.

- *Prioritisation.* Prioritising loved ones enhances our lives, nurturing emotional bonds through quality time and rendering those shared moments utterly precious.

- *Flow.* The concept of 'flow' guides us, prompting the pursuit of activities that captivate our focus, transporting us to a realm where time dances with abandon.

- *Gratitude.* Gratitude, a powerful elixir, lets us relish the simple joys and infuses our days with a positive glow, crafting unforgettable memories.

- *Balance.* A delicate balance between work, personal time, and leisure ensures that our presence in any given moment remains steadfast and complete, free from the burdens of overcommitment or excessive multitasking.

- *Positivity.* Embracing a positive mindset, coupled with an optimistic approach to challenges, turns tasks into enjoyable endeavours, reducing the perception of time's passage.
- *Stress management.* Managing stress and practising relaxation techniques keep us grounded and centred, allowing us to bask in the richness of the present.

Indeed, living in this extraordinary manner is a journey, requiring patience and dedication, but the rewards are boundless—a life that exudes fulfilment and joy, where time soars with delight, leaving behind a tapestry of treasured memories that endure for eternity. This emotional and psychological experience offers a departure from the conventional perception of time, leading to transformative moments. Just as time travel in science fiction opens up new possibilities, embracing each moment entirely lets us delve into the depths of our emotions, passions, and connections, unearthing the richness of our existence. It grants us the ability to savour the extraordinary aspects of life, turning the ordinary into the extraordinary, as we journey through the marvels of the present.

Mastering the Mind and Nurturing the Self

The mind should be a tool that serves the individual's will and decisions, rather than one that controls or overpowers the individuals. When the mind becomes the master, it may lead to various challenges. For example, overthinking or excessive worrying can hinder decision-making and cause unnecessary stress. On the other hand, when the mind is the servant, it obeys the individual's direction, allowing them to stay focused, make rational choices, and maintain emotional balance.

Holistic individuals have a profound understanding of the interconnectedness between their mind, body, and spirit. They view their minds as powerful tools, but they don't let their minds dictate their every action or emotion. Instead, they master their minds by cultivating self-awareness, mindfulness, and emotional intelligence.

By being the masters of their minds, they are able to observe their thoughts and emotions without being overwhelmed or controlled by them. They can make conscious decisions and respond to situations with clarity and balance. This empowers them to break free from negative thought patterns, fears, and anxieties.

Holistic individuals practise various techniques like meditation, yoga, or mindfulness exercises to train their minds and increase their mental resilience. They also prioritise self-care, maintain healthy relationships, and engage in activities that promote personal growth and fulfilment. By being the masters of their minds, they embrace change and adapt to life's challenges with resilience and grace. This sense of mastery fosters in them a deep sense of contentment, inner peace, and an overall sense of well-being.

Parallels Between Human Vitality and Car Longevity

Just as a symphony of precision and expertise unfolds in a world-class manufacturing company, where each car part is meticulously crafted and seamlessly integrated, so too does the marvel of human development take shape within the sanctuary of a mother's womb. With the finesse of a master artisan, the genetic blueprint guides the orchestrated emergence of organs—a crescendo of neural tubes, beating hearts, and budding limbs. Each stage witnesses, as in a precisely engineered assembly line, the creation of intricate systems that reflect the very essence of precision and quality. Sensory symphonies of eyes and ears, the grand finale of a fully matured foetal period, and the meticulous focus on life-sustaining lung development mirror the meticulous attention lavished upon crafting the most exquisite automobile. Just as a car is an engineering marvel, the formation of a human being is the pinnacle of biological craftsmanship, an opulent testament to the artistry of nature itself.

In the realms of life's grand creation and the crafting of mechanical marvels, proper care and maintenance resonates as a shared principle. Just as a car's optimal performance is an orchestration of diligent servicing, whereby engines are fine-tuned and parts are kept in harmonious sync, so too must we conduct ourselves as caretakers of our biological machinery. From infancy to adulthood, each stage mirrors a pit stop, demanding meticulous attention and nurturing. Just as a car's oil change ensures smooth functioning, nourishing our minds and bodies with knowledge and sustenance lubricates the wheels of our personal journey. As a skilled mechanic ensures that every component thrives, we must ensure for ourselves a life of wellness by tending to emotional engines, fostering relationships, and fuelling ourselves with positivity. Just as a car's longevity depends on vigilant care, our vitality depends on our self-care practices.

Indeed, life's journey unveils its magnificence when we become skilled mechanics for our own selves. Just as an artisan cherishes the masterpiece they sculpt, we must lovingly nurture our physical and emotional beings. Like an adept mechanic fine-tuning a grand automobile, we must harmonise body and mind, ensuring every note of our existence resonates in perfect cadence. With the tools of self-awareness and self-care, we can sculpt our well-being, crafting a life that hums with vitality.

Self-actualisation

Self-actualisation, the pinnacle of Abraham Maslow's hierarchy of needs, symbolises the realisation of one's fullest potential and the ultimate level of psychological development. At this stage, individuals engage in an intrapersonal competition, seeking perfection through self-reliance and self-improvement. Self-actualisation marks the culmination of one's personal growth journey, where one identifies and achieves individual milestones, consistently assessing one's progress and strategically planning one's professional development. Striving for a multitude of accomplishments in their chosen fields of interest or expertise, individuals may attain peak performance, showcasing remarkable skills and abilities honed through the lessons learnt from their most significant experiences.

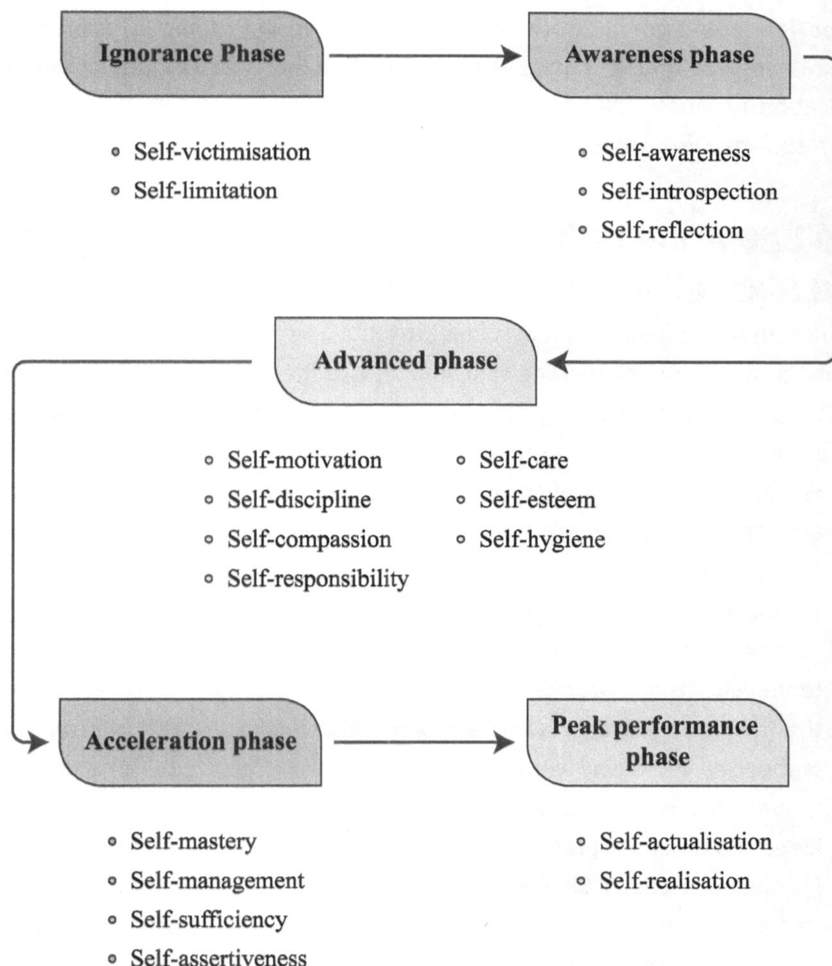

Holistic Entrepreneurs

Holistic entrepreneurs exhibit a unique blend of qualities and strategies that propel them to greatness. They are visionary thinkers, capable of identifying unmet needs and pioneering innovative solutions. Market research and customer-centricity are their guiding principles, enabling them to create products or services that resonate with their audience. These entrepreneurs embrace risk and adversity with resilience, viewing failures as stepping stones to success. Effective communication and leadership skills allow them to inspire and lead talented teams. They maintain a long-term vision built on meticulous planning while also staying grounded in ethical and socially responsible practices. Their ability to adapt, learn, and continuously improve, combined with financial acumen and a keen sense of timing, equips them for sustainable success. Ultimately, their dedication to measuring and analysing performance ensures they remain agile and responsive in a constantly evolving business landscape.

The Spectrum of Humanity: Unveiling the Feminine and Masculine Elements Within Us

The notion of feminine and masculine attributes, irrespective of one's gender, is grounded in the understanding that human qualities transcend specific gender identities. It's imperative to grasp that these characteristics are not confined to any particular gender; they exist within each of us, albeit in varying degrees.

- Feminine aspects: In every individual, regardless of gender, there resides a reservoir of tender yet potent qualities often associated with femininity. These include the profound capacity for deep empathy, which results in a soothing presence; intuition, which serves as a compass, guiding decision-making with inner wisdom, akin to a beacon in the darkness; nurturing tendencies that naturally emerge as we extend care to others, akin to the loving embrace of a mother; and collaboration, which is instinctively embedded in the way we value connections and aspire to build communities grounded in cooperation. Through us, creativity flows, birthing imaginative ideas and artistic expressions that adorn the world with vibrant hues.

- Masculine aspects: Simultaneously, the presence of masculine attributes transcends the confines of gender, manifesting within each of us. Assertiveness empowers us with the confidence to make decisions and take charge when required, akin to a resolute leader guiding a team. Logical thinking becomes a cornerstone of our approach, facilitating the dissection of problems, the discovery of solutions, and engagement in critical analysis. Independence beckons us to be self-reliant, to seize initiative, and to chart our own course with unyielding determination. Strength and resilience surface, enabling us to navigate life's challenges with composure and unwavering resolve. Goal-oriented inclinations propel us to establish objectives, pursue them, and relish the satisfaction of achievement.

These qualities coexist within every individual, forming an intricately beautiful mosaic of human nature. Embracing both these facets, feminine and masculine, is pivotal to attaining a balanced and holistic existence. By celebrating this diversity of traits, we unlock the potential to navigate life's complexities with grace, wisdom, and the entire spectrum of human capabilities. This odyssey towards self-understanding is a profound pursuit of holistic completeness.

In the realm of wholeness, extraordinary individuals stand tall like majestic pillars of light, radiating an aura of vibrancy that captivates all who encounter them.

Their journey begins with a celebration of nourishment. They feast on a bountiful spread of wholesome foods, each bite a source of vitality. They are culinary artists, crafting meals that not only nurture their physical well-being but also spark joy in every taste bud.

The senses become their enchanted companions, each one a magical gateway to the world's wonders. They embark on a quest for fitness, well-being, and a sacred union of mind and body. They dance under moonlit skies, flow like water in yoga's embrace, and meditate amidst ancient trees. This alchemy of exercise transforms their spirits, leaving them energised and serene, and ignites the spark of inspiration within.

Like magicians of emotion, they wield the power of self-awareness to tame the tempests within. Their hearts are vessels of courage, able to navigate the turbulent waters of joy, love, grief, and anger with grace. They embrace each emotion, knowing that through this alchemical process, they forge a deeper connection with their true selves.

Their holistic sanctuary glows with health, with every fibre of their being thriving in unity. They cherish the temple of the body, a mosaic of sacred parts that intertwine in harmony. With a gentle touch and attentive care, they honour the divine sanctum that houses their soul.

They weave their dreams with determination, their purpose not a mere mirage but a guiding star that lights their path. They kindle the fire of their passions and share their light, illuminating the lives of others with their joy and wisdom. With every gesture of kindness, they sprinkle stardust across the tapestry of humanity. They extend a helping hand, offer words of encouragement. Their compassion knows no bounds, and they know that even the smallest act of kindness can create a ripple that transforms the world. Within the treasury of their hearts, they discover the true meaning of abundance. They lavish love upon themselves and others, knowing that true wealth lies not in material possessions but in the richness of experiences, the currency of gratitude, and the gemstones of connection. As leaders, they ascend with grace, their footsteps resonating with empathy and compassion. They listen like oracles, attuned to the needs of those around them, and guide others towards their own wholeness. Their presence creates a nurturing haven where growth flourishes and brilliance blooms.

They dance with the cosmos, embracing the sacred dance of authenticity. In a world that craves conformity, they unfurl their wings of uniqueness, refusing to be anything other than themselves. They are the living embodiment of authenticity's enchantment, and their radiance is an invitation for others to embrace their own true selves.

As they stride through the meadows of life, they encounter storms and shadows, but they are not swayed. Their roots run deep like those of ancient trees, standing firm in the face of adversity. They are resilient, turning challenges into stepping stones and transforming darkness into light.

In the gallery of their minds, they paint with colours of curiosity and open-mindedness. Their thirst for knowledge is insatiable, and they seek wisdom from every corner of existence. They embrace the kaleidoscope of perspectives, knowing that it is through the prism of diversity that the rainbow of understanding emerges.

As caretakers of the Earth, they coexist in harmony with the elements. They bow to the majesty of nature, recognising their role as guardians of that which nourishes and sustains them. They live in symbiosis with the planet, making mindful choices to preserve its beauty for the generations yet to come. They are the keepers of balance, the seekers of truth, and the architects of a harmonious world. They embody a profound respect for humanity and the environment, abstaining from adulteration or contamination of food.

They eschew violence, for they comprehend the principles of anger management, opting for peaceful resolutions even in the face of adversity. Their approach to parenting is a testament to their wisdom; they nurture children with a holistic understanding, fostering their growth across all the dimensions of being.

They channel their energy towards constructive contributions to society. Through volunteering, active community involvement, and the passionate advocacy of social causes, they play a pivotal role in effecting positive change.

Holistic individuals extend their principles of respect and mindfulness to every aspect of their daily lives, ensuring they never engage in un civilactions such as violating traffic rules, jumping queues, or showing disrespect to elders and children.

Holistic individuals abstain from creating excessively violent movies due to their awareness that such content, while fictional, has the potential to impact millions of viewers by perpetuating a culture of violence. Filmmakers and actors may justify depicting violence by claiming it reflects real-world events, but they often fail to recognise the broader impact it can have on audiences worldwide. Similarly, creators of violent video games may argue that their content is a form of artistic expression, yet they overlook the potential influence on players, particularly younger audiences, who are likely to be affected by the content they consume.

Holistic individuals embody a growth mindset, recognising that learning and evolution are lifelong pursuits. They embrace fresh concepts and perspectives, for they understand that stagnation is antithetical to holistic living. Resilience, not provocation, defines their response to challenges. They cherish not only physical health but also the intricate interplay of mental, emotional, and spiritual well-being.

Rather than embarking on grandiose endeavours to change the entire world, the truly profound and impactful approach lies in the transformation of individuals. The ripple effect is immeasurable. It spreads outward, touching families, communities, nations, and eventually, the world. By focusing on the transformation of individuals, we set in motion a wave of change that has the power to reshape the very foundations of our existence. It's not about changing the world all at once, but about nurturing a collective consciousness that, over time, will inevitably lead to a world that reflects these ideals in every facet of life.

Key takeaways: Personal transformation as holistic individuals is possible at any stage of life, through the practice of self-love, self-awareness and self-reflection by

- **Ensuring the proper ingestion of nutrients**
- **Facilitating the efficient excretion of body wastes**
- **Cultivating constructive thoughts**
- **Diminishing destructive thoughts**

'It is never too late to be what you might have been.'

\- George Eliot

Comprehensive Annual Fitness Checklist

Body Metrics

- Body weight: _______ lbs/kg
- BMI: _______
- Waist circumference: _______ inches/cm

Cardiovascular Health

- Resting heart rate: _______ bpm
- Average daily steps: _______ steps/day
- Ave.running distance: _______ miles/km
- Mountain climber exercise:_______ seconds
- How long you can hold your breath: _______seconds

Strength and Muscular Endurance

- Muscle mass: _______ lbs/kg
- Max push-ups in one set: _______
- Max pull-ups in one set: _______
- Weightlifting goals (if any):

Functional Fitness

- Max plank time: _______ seconds
- Max squats: _______
- Deadlifts: _______ lbs/kg
- Max lunges: _______

Flexibility Goals

- Touch toes without bending knees
- Hold a seated forward bend
- Hip flexibility for better squat posture
- Butterfly stretch
- Neck flexibility to comfortably look over both shoulders
- Shoulder rotation

Endurance Activities

- Max cycling distance: _______ miles/km
- Max swimming distance: _______ miles/km
- Marathon: ___ | ___ (miles/km | hours)

Mindfulness and Mental Health

- Meditation practice: _______ minutes/day (average)
- Yoga:_______ minutes/day (average)
- Mudras:_______ minutes/day (average)

Health Metrics

- Blood pressure: _______ mmHg
- Blood sugar: ______ mg/dl
- Carbs: _______ grams
- Protein: _______ grams
- Fats: _______ grams

Additional Goals

- Eye vision:
- Teeth:
- Ear:

Note: maintaining a lifelong comprehensive annual fitness checklists serves as a valuable tool for continuous self-evaluation and personal well-being.

Comprehensive Self-Assessment Algorithm for Overall Well-Being

Self-Reflection and Emotional Awareness Algorithm

- Set aside dedicated time for self-reflection (e.g. learn from midlife crisis)
- Assess emotional state and reactions to various situations (e.g. traffic, deadlines)
- Gauge emotional intelligence through self-assessment quizzes (e.g. EQ tests)

Physical Health Algorithm

- Monitor physical health, including sleep, exercise, and nutrition (e.g. by tracking daily steps)
- Consider practices that promote overall physical wellness (e.g. yoga, meditation)

Mental Health Algorithm

- Evaluate mental well-being and stress levels (e.g. susceptibility to sudden provocation)
- Reflect on activities that positively impact mental health (e.g. practising gratitude)
- Adjust strategies to support mental well-being (e.g. seeking therapy if needed)

Strengths, Weaknesses, and Goals Algorithm

- Identify strengths, talents, and areas of expertise (e.g. problem-solving, creativity)
- Evaluate weaknesses that might hinder progress (e.g. time management skills)
- Review personal and professional goals and assess progress (e.g. career milestones, fitness goals)

Lifestyle and Time Management Algorithm

- Reflect on how time and energy are managed daily (e.g. work, leisure, sleep)
- Evaluate if activities align with priorities and well-being (e.g. spending time with loved ones)
- Adjust schedules to accommodate self-care and personal growth (e.g. exercise routines, learning new skills)

Interpersonal Relationships Algorithm
- Reflect on the quality of relationships with family, friends, and colleagues (e.g. regular check-ins)
- Assess communication skills and ability to build meaningful connections (e.g. active listening)
- Adjust interactions to strengthen relationships and resolve conflicts (e.g. effective communication)

Communication Skills Algorithm
- Reflect on the quality of communication with others (e.g. clarity, empathy)
- Assess listening skills and ability to convey ideas effectively(e.g. information recall)
- Adjust communication style to foster better understanding and connection (e.g. use 'we' language.

Financial Health and Planning Algorithm
- Review financial goals, budget, and spending habits (e.g. creating a monthly budget)
- Assess financial well-being and identify areas for improvement (e.g. reducing unnecessary expenses)
- Plan for savings and investments to secure a stable financial future (e.g. SIP)

Personal Growth and Development Algorithm
- Reflect on ongoing learning and skill enhancement efforts (e.g. taking online courses).
- Evaluate progress in personal and professional development (e.g. improved public speaking skills)
- Adjust strategies to continue learning and adapting to change (e.g. seeking out mentorship)

Life Satisfaction and Self-actualisation Algorithm
- Regularly rate overall life satisfaction and happiness (e.g. on a scale of 1 to 10)
- Assess activities and experiences that contribute to well-being (e.g. hobbies, spending time in nature)
- Assess peak performance and full potential (e.g. world record, record growth)
- Make adjustments to enhance overall life satisfaction (e.g. dedicating more time to enjoyable activities)